Published by
Rupa Publications India Pvt. Ltd 2025
7/16, Ansari Road, Daryaganj
New Delhi 110002

Sales centres:
Bengaluru Chennai
Hyderabad Jaipur Kathmandu
Kolkata Mumbai Prayagraj

Copyright © Rupa Publications India Pvt. Ltd 2025

The views and opinions expressed in this book are the authors' own and the facts are as reported by him which have been verified to the extent possible, and the publishers are not in any way liable for the same.

All rights reserved.
No part of this publication may be reproduced, transmitted, or stored in a retrieval system, in any form or by any means, electronic, mechanical, photocopying, recording or otherwise, without the prior permission of the publisher.

Photo Source: Wikimedia Commons and Philstar

ISBN: 978-93-6156-927-2

First impression 2025

10 9 8 7 6 5 4 3 2 1

The moral right of the author has been asserted.

Printed in India

This book is sold subject to the condition that it shall not, by way of trade or otherwise, be lent, resold, hired out, or otherwise circulated, without the publisher's prior consent, in any form of binding or cover other than that in which it is published.

CONTENTS

Introduction		5
1.	The History of Shooting Sports	8

SECTION ONE
GETTING STARTED

2.	Understanding Shooting Sports	18
3.	Equipment and Gear	34
4.	Shooting Stance and Movement	44

SECTION TWO
THE BASICS

5.	Basic Shooting Techniques and Combinations	58
6.	Defensive Techniques in Shooting Sports	70
7.	Range Time and Drills	80

SECTION THREE
CONDITIONING AND TRAINING

8. Mental Conditioning and Focus on Shooting Sports — 90
9. Physical Conditioning for Shooters — 103
10. Nutrition and Diet for Shooting Sports — 112

SECTION FOUR
ADVANCED TECHNIQUES AND STRATEGY

11. Precision Mastery: Advanced Shooting Skills — 120

SECTION FIVE
THE ART OF COMPETITIVE MARKSMANSHIP

12. Preparing for Your First Shooting Competition — 126
13. Analyzing Competitions and Learning from Experience — 136
14. The Future of Shooting Sports — 141
15. Nurturing the Next Olympic Shooter — 146
16. Filipino Olympians in Shooting Sports — 150

List of Olympic Medalists in Shooting (2008–2024) — 154

INTRODUCTION

SHOOTING IS MORE THAN JUST PULLING A TRIGGER—it's a discipline that blends precision, control, and a deep understanding of physics. Whether using firearms, airguns, or bows, shooting sports challenges individuals to hone their accuracy, speed, and composure under pressure. From the quiet solitude of target shooting to the high-stakes drama of competitive matches, the art of shooting requires a steady hand, a focused mind, and an unwavering commitment to safety.

This book aims to guide you through the diverse world of shooting sports, offering insights into its storied history, the various equipment and techniques used, and the mental and physical conditioning needed to excel. At its heart, shooting is a test of precision and consistency. Each shot involves a careful orchestration of stance, breath, aim, and trigger control—each movement purposeful and deliberate.

Shooting sports have evolved into a global phenomenon; from Olympic rifle events to dynamic practical shooting, the sport is as much about personal mastery as it is about competition.

THE EVOLUTION OF SHOOTING SPORTS

From the use of bows and crossbows in medieval warfare to the emergence of firearms in the 14th century, the evolution of shooting sports reflects advancements in weapon technology and the human desire for precision and competition. The transition from practical use to sport began in the 19th century with the establishment of shooting clubs and the standardization of rules, leading to the formalization of competitions.

The modern era of shooting sports includes a variety of disciplines such as rifle, pistol, and shotgun shooting, each with its own set of rules and equipment specifications. The sport has produced legendary marksmen like Ralf Schumann and Kim Rhode, who have set records and won multiple Olympic medals. These athletes not only showcase the physical skill and concentration required in shooting sports but also emphasize the importance of mental focus and control. As the sport continues to evolve, innovations such as laser rifles and electronic scoring systems are shaping the future of competitive shooting.

WHY LEARN SHOOTING SPORTS?

Whether you're a beginner, a recreational shooter, or an aspiring competitor, learning shooting sports offers a range of benefits. Physically, shooting sports improve hand-eye coordination, fine motor skills, and focus. It is a discipline that requires precision and control, engaging both the body and mind in a unique way. For those looking to challenge themselves, the sport offers various disciplines like rifle, pistol, and shotgun shooting, each with its own set of skills and techniques.

Beyond the physical benefits, shooting sports foster mental toughness and discipline. The ability to concentrate under pressure, the patience to improve shot by shot, and the resilience to handle competition are valuable skills that translate beyond the shooting range. Shooting sports also instill a sense of responsibility, safety, and respect for firearms, which are crucial aspects of the sport.

This guide is designed to take you through the essentials of shooting sports. From understanding the basics of safety and equipment to mastering shooting techniques and competition strategies, you'll gain comprehensive knowledge to enhance your skills. Whether you're aiming for personal improvement or competitive success, this guide will provide the foundation you need to excel in shooting sports.

Embark on this journey into the world of shooting sports, where each shot tests your accuracy, every competition sharpens your resolve, and every day at the range builds confidence and respect for this timeless sport. Welcome to the challenge and excitement of shooting sports, where precision meets passion.

1

THE HISTORY OF SHOOTING SPORTS

ORIGINS OF SHOOTING SPORTS

Shooting sports have a rich history that dates back several centuries, evolving from hunting and military training into formalized competitive and recreational activities. The earliest forms of target shooting can be traced to the late medieval period, when archery contests were common in Europe. However, the advent of firearms in the 15th century marked a significant turning point, as people began to test their skills with muskets and rifles.

In Great Britain, the National Rifle Association was established in 1859, promoting rifle shooting among volunteer corps. This led to the development of various shooting clubs and competitions across the country. In the United States, shooting competitions have been popular since colonial times, with events like turkey shoots serving as early examples. These informal contests laid the groundwork for the organized sport of shooting we see today.

The modern shooting sport began to take shape in the late 19th century, spurred by advancements in firearm technology and the establishment of standardized rules.

Throughout its history, shooting has adapted to include a variety of disciplines, from rifle and pistol to shotgun and airgun events, each with unique rules and formats. Today, shooting sports are governed internationally by bodies such as the International Shooting Sport Federation (ISSF), which ensures consistency and fairness in competitions worldwide. The sport continues to attract participants of all ages and abilities, celebrating both individual achievement and team cooperation in the pursuit of excellence in marksmanship.

EVOLUTION OF THE SPORT

The modern sport of shooting began to take shape in Europe during the late 19th century, building on traditions of marksmanship that date back centuries. Initially, shooting was used primarily for hunting and military training, but as firearms became more advanced and accessible, shooting evolved into a competitive sport. Early competitions were often informal and lacked standardized rules, with participants using a wide range of firearms and equipment. These events were typically held in open fields or shooting galleries, attracting spectators who were eager to witness displays of precision and skill.

The first significant step towards formalizing shooting sports came with the establishment of the National Rifle Association in Britain in 1859, which aimed to promote rifle shooting among the country's volunteer forces. This was followed by the formation of similar organizations in other countries, including the United States, where shooting competitions quickly gained popularity. The need for standardized rules and fair play led to the creation of the International Shooting Sport Federation (ISSF) in 1907, which began to oversee and regulate shooting competitions worldwide.

Laser clay shooting, Cricklade Show

Shooting sports made their debut in the Olympic Games in 1896, featuring five disciplines that tested the accuracy and precision of competitors. Over the years, the sport has expanded to include a variety of events, such as rifle, pistol, shotgun, and airgun competitions. The introduction of standardized rules, such as those governing the type of firearms, target specifications, and scoring systems, helped to legitimize shooting as a competitive sport. Safety measures were also implemented, with a strong emphasis on firearm safety and responsible handling.

THE HISTORY OF SHOOTING SPORTS

1960 Israel marksmanship team to the Olympics and their trainer.
Left to right: Hanan Crystal, trainer Izzy Gilam and Raffi Peles

The 20th century saw significant advancements in the technology and techniques used in shooting sports. Innovations such as the development of more precise and reliable firearms, electronic scoring systems, and the inclusion of air guns allowed the sport to grow and attract a wider audience. Additionally, the establishment of weight categories and equipment divisions ensured fair competition among participants, catering to a diverse range of skill levels and physical capabilities.

As shooting sports continued to evolve, they also faced challenges, including public concerns about gun safety and the sport's association with violence. In response, governing bodies like the ISSF and various national shooting organizations have worked to promote the sport's positive aspects, such as discipline, focus, and the importance of safety. These organizations also play a crucial role in

OLYMPIC SERIES: SHOOTING

maintaining the integrity of the sport by enforcing rules and regulations designed to protect participants and ensure fair play.

The continued evolution of shooting sports, with new events and technologies, ensures its place as a dynamic and enduring form of competition.

FAMOUS SHOOTERS AND ICONIC COMPETITIONS

Throughout its history, shooting sports have produced some of the most legendary and celebrated athletes in the world of precision sports. These shooters have not only excelled in their disciplines but have also inspired generations of enthusiasts and athletes with their remarkable achievements and dedication.

Stamp of India—2016

One of the most renowned shooters of all time is Ralf Schumann, a German pistol shooter who is widely regarded as one of the greatest in Olympic history. Schumann dominated the 25-meter rapid-fire pistol event, winning three Olympic gold medals and one silver across five Olympic Games from 1988 to 2008. Known for his extraordinary precision and quick reflexes, Schumann set multiple world records during his career and became a symbol of consistency and excellence in the sport.

Kim Rhode is another iconic figure in shooting sports, known for her incredible versatility and success across multiple Olympic Games. An American shooter specializing in skeet and double trap, Rhode has won six Olympic medals, including three golds, across six consecutive Games from 1996 to 2016—a record in itself. Her remarkable ability to adapt to different shooting disciplines and her consistent performance over the decades has made her one of the most celebrated athletes in shooting sports history.

Marine Corps Trials shooting competition

Sergey Martynov, a Belarusian rifle shooter, is celebrated for his prowess in the 50-meter prone rifle event. Martynov won gold at the 2012 London Olympics with a perfect score of 600, a feat that highlighted his exceptional focus and precision. Over his career, Martynov accumulated numerous world records and medals, solidifying his status as one of the greatest marksmen in the history of the sport.

Another legendary shooter is Niccolò Campriani of Italy, who excelled in rifle shooting. Campriani won three Olympic gold medals in the 10-meter air rifle and 50-meter rifle three positions, demonstrating exceptional versatility and control across events. Known for his strategic approach and mental fortitude, Campriani's achievements have made him a role model for aspiring shooters worldwide.

Jin Jong-oh of South Korea is considered one of the greatest pistol shooters in Olympic history. With four Olympic gold medals and two silvers in the 50-meter pistol and 10-meter air pistol events, Jin's success is a testament to his incredible discipline and technical skill. His ability to perform under pressure and his numerous world records have cemented his legacy as a shooting sports icon.

In addition to these iconic athletes, shooting sports have seen countless other legends, such as Rajmond Debevec, known for his longevity and success in rifle events over nine Olympic Games; Vasily Borisov, a Soviet Union shooter who dominated rifle shooting in the 1950s and 60s; and Abhinav Bindra, who became India's first individual Olympic gold medalist in 10-meter air rifle. These shooters and their outstanding performances in international competitions have shaped the history of shooting sports and left an enduring legacy on the sport.

Shooting Tournament at the 1900 Olympic Games in Paris

India has also produced several celebrated shooters who have left their mark on the international stage. Among them, Abhinav Bindra stands out as a pioneering figure in Indian sports. He made history by becoming India's first individual Olympic gold medalist in the 10-meter air rifle event at the 2008 Beijing Olympics. His victory not only elevated the status of shooting sports in India but also inspired a generation of young athletes to pursue excellence in this field.

Another notable Indian shooter is Rajyavardhan Singh Rathore, who won a silver medal in double trap shooting at the 2004 Athens Olympics, marking India's first-ever Olympic shooting medal. His achievement brought significant attention to shooting sports in India and paved the way for future athletes.

Gagan Narang, a prolific shooter specializing in the

10-meter air rifle, won the bronze medal at the 2012 London Olympics, adding to his impressive tally of World Cup and Commonwealth Games medals. His consistent performances have made him a prominent figure in Indian shooting.

Another distinguished Indian shooter is Jitu Rai, known for his success in pistol events. Rai has won multiple medals at the World Championships, Asian Games, and Commonwealth Games, showcasing his versatility and precision in both 10-meter air pistol and 50-meter pistol events.

Staff Sgt. Mowrer and James Hall competed in 10m air pistol at the 2020 Olympics

These Indian shooters, along with others like Anjali Bhagwat, Manu Bhaker, and Saurabh Chaudhary, have not only excelled in their respective disciplines but have also contributed to the growing popularity and success of shooting sports in India. Their dedication and achievements continue to inspire aspiring shooters across the nation.

SECTION ONE

GETTING STARTED

2

UNDERSTANDING SHOOTING SPORTS

WHAT IS SHOOTING SPORTS?

Shooting sports encompass a diverse array of activities where participants use firearms, airguns, or bows to hit targets with utmost accuracy and precision. This discipline requires a unique blend of physical skill and mental fortitude, making it distinct from many other sports. Unlike those that demand raw physical strength or endurance, shooting is more about the steady hand, sharp focus, and the ability to maintain composure under pressure. It's the perfect amalgamation of physical mechanics and mental strategy, where every shot counts, and every miss is a lesson in patience and control.

The primary objective in shooting sports is simple yet challenging: to strike the target as accurately as possible. Competitors aim to score points by hitting designated areas, with bullseyes or inner rings awarding higher scores. Achieving this requires mastering various techniques such as proper stance, grip, and breathing control. Whether it's precision target shooting with pistols, rifles, or dynamic shooting with shotguns, each discipline demands a unique set of skills and an unwavering focus on precision.

Shooting events are conducted in carefully controlled environments—ranges that can be indoor or outdoor. These ranges are designed to simulate various shooting conditions, with distances that vary according to the type of competition. For instance, air rifle events typically involve 10-meter targets, while rifle and shotgun disciplines can see distances stretching to 50 meters or beyond. Courses may present stationary or moving targets, demanding not just accuracy but also quick reflexes and adaptability.

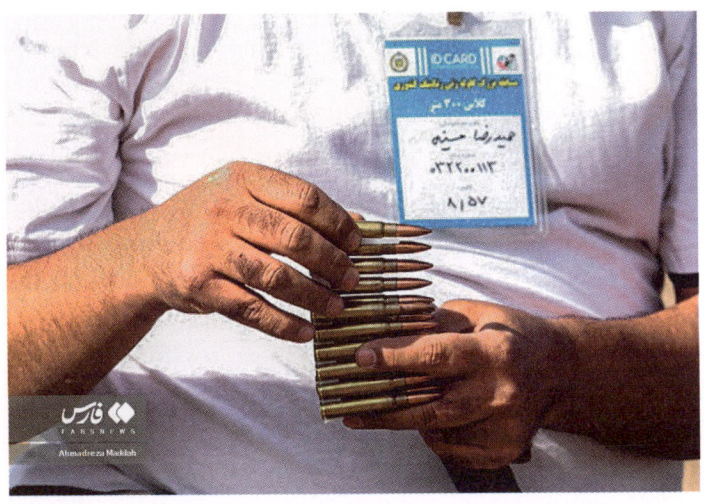

A strip of rifle ammunition at a national shooting competition in Shiraz

Shooting sports are often called "the art of precision," as they require a delicate balance between physical execution and mental calmness. Shooters must be proficient with their equipment, managing variables such as wind, shooting angles, and bullet trajectory. They need to make instantaneous adjustments, especially in competitive scenarios where even a slight miscalculation can lead to missed opportunities. In high-stakes competitions, controlling nerves becomes as crucial as technical skill, turning each event into a mental game as much as a physical one.

THE BASIC RULES AND REGULATIONS

Understanding the rules and regulations of shooting sports is crucial, not only for competitors but also for those who wish to engage as enthusiasts or spectators. These rules are designed to ensure fairness, safety, and the integrity of the sport.

1. The Range

Shooting competitions are held in specific, regulated ranges, which are meticulously designed to guarantee the safety of all participants and spectators. Depending on the discipline—whether pistol, rifle, or shotgun—the layout of the range can differ. Common features include safety barriers, designated firing lines, and shooting booths, all adhering to strict protocols to minimize risks. Participants must follow exacting safety measures, with clear guidelines on handling weapons, maintaining focus on the targets, and abiding by range commands.

2. Distances and Targets

Targets and their corresponding distances are tailored to each shooting discipline. For example, air rifle events often take place at 10 meters, whereas disciplines like trap or skeet shooting involve targets at distances of 15 to 50 meters or more. Targets themselves come in various forms—some are stationary, others moving, and they can be circular bullseyes or silhouette shapes, each designed to test a shooter's accuracy and reaction time in different ways.

3. Scoring

Points in shooting sports are determined by the precision of each shot. Targets are typically divided into scoring zones, with the highest points awarded for hits closest to the center or bullseye. Some competitions utilize highly detailed scoring systems that measure shots down to the nearest millimeter, while others may employ simpler methods, such as counting the number of hits within designated zones. Consistency and precision are key, and even the slightest deviation can significantly impact a competitor's overall score.

4. Shoot-offs and Ties

In the event of a tie, shoot-offs are used to determine the winner. These extra rounds heighten the tension, requiring competitors to hit increasingly difficult targets under timed conditions. The exact rules for shoot-offs can vary by discipline, but the essence remains the same: a battle of nerves and precision where only the most composed will emerge victorious.

5. Fouls and Safety Violations

Safety is the cornerstone of shooting sports. Strict rules govern every aspect of firearm and ammunition handling to prevent accidents. Common violations include misfires, mishandling of equipment, or failure to follow range commands. Consequences for such infractions can be severe, ranging from warnings to disqualification, depending on the nature and gravity of the offense. Competitors are expected to exhibit the highest standards of safety and discipline at all times.

6. Equipment

Competitors must use approved equipment that meets specific standards to ensure fairness and safety. This includes firearms or airguns of regulated specifications, along with mandatory protective gear such as eyewear and ear protection. In some disciplines, specialized shooting jackets or gloves are worn to enhance stability and performance. Equipment checks are routine, and any discrepancies can result in penalties or disqualification.

7. Referee's Role

Referees or range officers play a critical role in maintaining the safety and integrity of the competition. They oversee the event, ensuring that all participants adhere strictly to the rules. Their responsibilities include managing the scoring process, monitoring equipment compliance, and addressing any disputes that arise, such as challenges to scores. Referees have the authority to pause or halt the competition if unsafe behavior is observed, underscoring the importance of their role in the sport.

Abhinav Bindra and Gagan Narang won gold in the 10m Air Rifle Men's Pair at the 2010 Commonwealth Games in Delhi

THE ROLE OF SHOOTING SPORTS ORGANIZATIONS (ISSF, NRA, IPSC, ETC.)

Shooting sports are globally recognized for their emphasis on precision, discipline, and safety. The sport is governed by several major organizations that establish the standards, rules, and regulations for competition, ensuring that athletes compete fairly and safely. The most prominent organizations in the world of shooting sports include the International Shooting Sport Federation (ISSF), the National Rifle Association (NRA), the International Practical Shooting Confederation (IPSC), and the World Archery Federation (WA). These organizations are crucial in maintaining the structure and integrity of shooting sports, providing frameworks for competition, and promoting the sport on an international scale.

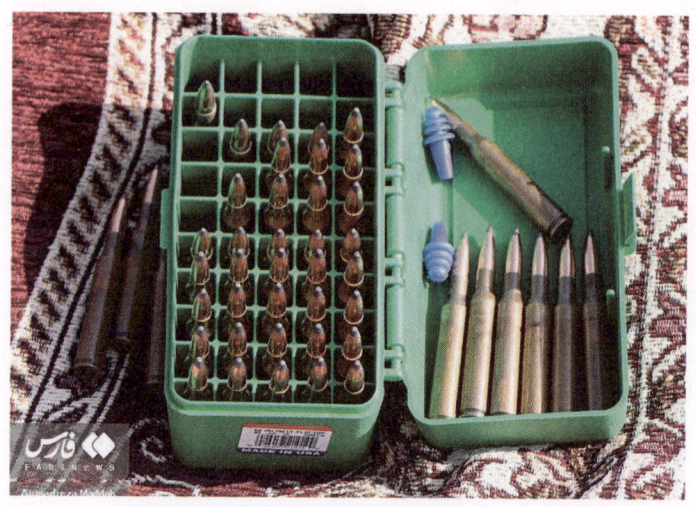

A green plastic ammunition box at a national shooting competition in Shiraz

1. International Shooting Sport Federation (ISSF)

Founded in 1907, the ISSF is the oldest and most influential organization in shooting sports, overseeing Olympic disciplines such as rifle, pistol, and shotgun events. The ISSF sets the international rules for these sports and governs competitions at the highest levels, including the Olympics, World Championships, and World Cups. It plays a pivotal role in standardizing equipment, scoring systems, and safety protocols. The ISSF is also responsible for promoting the sport globally, encouraging participation across all age groups and skill levels. Its commitment to innovation is evident in its adoption of electronic scoring systems and its efforts to enhance the spectator experience through live broadcasts and interactive platforms.

2. National Rifle Association (NRA)

Established in 1871, the NRA is one of the most prominent shooting sports organizations in the United States, with a significant influence on the development of rifle, pistol, and shotgun shooting disciplines. The NRA provides training, competition opportunities, and education on safe firearm handling. It sanctions numerous national competitions and has established a comprehensive ranking system for shooters of various skill levels. The NRA's contributions extend beyond competition, as it actively advocates for the rights of gun owners and promotes shooting sports as a safe and responsible recreational activity. The NRA's extensive network of clubs and ranges makes it a key player in fostering grassroots participation in shooting sports across the U.S.

3. International Practical Shooting Confederation (IPSC)

Founded in 1976, the IPSC governs the dynamic and rapidly growing discipline of practical shooting, which emphasizes speed, accuracy, and power. The IPSC's unique format includes stages that simulate real-world shooting scenarios, requiring competitors to navigate courses while engaging targets from various positions and distances. The IPSC sets the standards for competition safety, equipment, and scoring, with an emphasis on challenging athletes to think quickly and adapt to changing conditions. The IPSC's motto,

"Diligentia, Vis, Celeritas" (Accuracy, Power, Speed), reflects its philosophy of testing shooters' all-around abilities. The IPSC has a strong global presence, with member regions in over 100 countries, and regularly hosts regional, national, and world championship events.

A high-precision rifle equipped with a large scope at a national shooting competition in Shiraz

4. World Archery Federation (WA)

While primarily associated with archery, the World Archery Federation (formerly known as FITA) plays a significant role in the realm of shooting sports, particularly in events that involve bows and crossbows. Established in 1931, WA governs international archery competitions, including those at the Olympic level. It sets the rules for various archery disciplines, including target archery, field archery, and 3D archery, and promotes the sport through extensive youth programs and global development initiatives. The organization emphasizes fair play, safety, and the advancement of archery as both a competitive sport and a recreational activity.

These organizations collectively play a vital role in the governance and promotion of shooting sports worldwide. They provide the structure and standards necessary for fair competition, ensure that safety protocols are strictly adhered to, and work tirelessly to expand the sport's reach and popularity.

DISCIPLINES AND CATEGORIES IN SHOOTING SPORTS

Shooting sports encompass a wide range of disciplines, each with its own unique set of rules, equipment, and skills required. From precision shooting with rifles and pistols to the fast-paced action of practical shooting, each discipline offers a distinct challenge to competitors. Understanding these categories is essential for appreciating the diversity and complexity of shooting sports.

1. Rifle Shooting

Rifle shooting is one of the core disciplines in shooting sports, with events that test a shooter's precision and control at various distances. Competitors use .22 caliber small-bore rifles or larger caliber rifles in events such as 10m Air Rifle, 50m Rifle 3 Positions, and 300m Rifle events. Shooters must maintain a steady hand and precise aim while standing, kneeling, or prone. Rifle shooting demands a high level of concentration, breath control, and the ability to remain calm under pressure. Events are held in both indoor and outdoor ranges, with conditions such as wind and light playing a significant role in outdoor competitions.

2. Pistol Shooting

Pistol shooting encompasses a variety of events, including 10m Air Pistol, 25m Rapid Fire Pistol, and 50m Pistol events. This discipline requires exceptional hand-eye coordination and the ability to maintain stability and control while shooting at targets from a standing position. Pistol shooters must master the art of trigger control and sight alignment, often with just one hand. The rapid fire events add a dynamic element, requiring shooters to engage multiple targets within a limited time frame, testing both speed and precision.

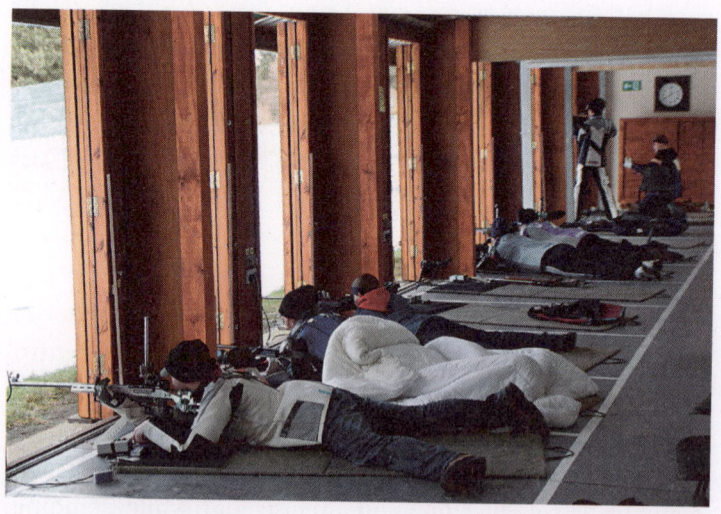

Competitors at the 2013 Isle of Man Easter Shooting Festival

3. Shotgun Shooting

Shotgun shooting is known for its dynamic nature, with disciplines such as Trap, Skeet, and Sporting Clays. In these events, competitors use 12-gauge shotguns to hit clay targets that are launched into the air at varying speeds and angles. Shotgun shooting tests a shooter's reflexes, timing, and ability to track moving targets. Each discipline presents its own set of challenges: Trap involves shooting targets launched away from the shooter, Skeet features targets crossing from side to side, and Sporting Clays simulate a variety of game bird hunting scenarios with targets launched in unpredictable patterns.

4. Practical Shooting

Practical shooting, governed by the IPSC, combines accuracy, power, and speed in a highly dynamic environment. Competitors navigate courses that require them to engage targets from multiple positions, often on the move and under time constraints. Courses are designed to mimic real-life scenarios, incorporating obstacles, moving targets, and varied shooting distances. Practical shooting is unique in its emphasis on strategy, as competitors must decide the most efficient way to complete the course while adhering to strict safety standards. Equipment in practical shooting can include pistols, rifles, and shotguns, each with specific divisions based on firearm type and modifications allowed.

5. Archery and Crossbow Shooting

While not involving firearms, archery and crossbow shooting are integral parts of shooting sports, emphasizing precision and control. Events range from traditional target archery to more complex formats like field archery and 3D archery, where competitors shoot at life-sized animal targets in natural settings. Crossbow shooting adds a modern twist to traditional archery, combining the challenge of accuracy with the mechanics of a crossbow. Both disciplines require excellent focus, steady hands, and the ability to adjust to environmental factors such as wind and distance.

6. Biathlon

Biathlon is a winter sport that combines cross-country skiing with rifle shooting, testing athletes' endurance, precision, and composure. Competitors ski over a course and stop at designated shooting ranges to hit targets from both standing and prone positions. Missing a target results in time penalties or additional skiing, making shooting accuracy a critical component of the sport. Biathlon is a test of physical fitness and shooting skill, requiring athletes to lower their heart rate rapidly after intense skiing to shoot accurately.

EQUIPMENT AND SAFETY STANDARDS IN SHOOTING SPORTS

Shooting sports require specialized equipment tailored to each discipline, and strict safety standards are in place to protect competitors, officials, and spectators. Understanding the equipment used and the safety measures enforced is essential for anyone involved in shooting sports, whether as a competitor, coach, or enthusiast.

UNDERSTANDING SHOOTING SPORTS

A shooting range during a national shooting competition in Shiraz

1. Firearms and Bows

The choice of firearm or bow depends on the specific discipline. Rifles, pistols, shotguns, and bows are all used in various formats, each with specific calibers or draw weights. For example, .22 caliber rifles are standard in Olympic rifle shooting, while 12-gauge shotguns are commonly used in skeet and trap shooting. Archers use recurve bows in Olympic events, while compound and traditional bows are used in other archery disciplines. Each piece of equipment must meet precise specifications set by the governing bodies, ensuring fairness and consistency in competition.

2. Protective Gear

Safety is a top priority in shooting sports, with protective gear being mandatory in many disciplines. Ear protection is essential in all firearms events to protect against the loud noise of gunfire, and eye protection is required to shield against potential debris or accidents. In practical shooting and other dynamic disciplines, competitors may also wear additional gear like shooting vests or gloves designed to enhance stability and comfort.

3. Safety Protocols

All shooting sports operate under strict safety protocols that govern the handling, loading, and firing of firearms or bows. Competitors are trained extensively in these protocols, which include keeping firearms unloaded until on the firing line, always pointing firearms downrange, and adhering to commands from range officers. Safety checks are conducted regularly to ensure that all equipment is functioning correctly and meets the required standards.

4. Range Safety and Layout

Shooting ranges are designed with safety as the foremost concern. Features such as bullet traps, safety barriers, and designated firing lines help contain shots and protect participants and spectators. Ranges are typically equipped with electronic scoring systems that allow for accurate and immediate feedback on performance, reducing the need for manual target handling. Outdoor ranges must also consider environmental factors, such as wind and lighting, which can affect shooting conditions.

Catalog of an exhibition of old sporting prints collected and for sale by Mr. Basil Dighton

5. Referees and Range Officers

Referees and range officers play a crucial role in maintaining the safety and integrity of shooting sports competitions. They are responsible for overseeing the event, enforcing rules, and ensuring that all safety protocols are followed.

3

EQUIPMENT AND GEAR

ESSENTIAL SHOOTING SPORTS GEAR: FIREARMS, AMMUNITION, PROTECTIVE GEAR, AND MORE

Shooting sports require a wide range of specialized equipment to ensure the safety of participants, enhance performance, and comply with the regulations of each discipline. The right gear not only protects the shooter but also optimizes accuracy, comfort, and control. This chapter provides a comprehensive guide to essential shooting sports gear, including firearms, ammunition, protective gear, and maintenance tools, along with tips on choosing, maintaining, and caring for your equipment.

1. Firearms

Purpose and Importance:

Firearms are the primary tools in shooting sports, with specific types designed for various disciplines such as rifle shooting, pistol shooting, and shotgun events. The choice of firearm significantly affects performance, as different models offer unique features tailored to precision, power, or speed.

Soldiers shoot double trap at Rio Olympic Games

Types of Firearms

- **Rifles:** Used in disciplines like 10m Air Rifle, 50m Prone Rifle, and biathlon. Rifles are known for their accuracy over varying distances, with configurations ranging from air rifles to high-caliber long-range rifles. They feature adjustable stocks, high-quality scopes, and customizable triggers to enhance precision.
- **Pistols:** Commonly used in events such as 10m Air Pistol, 25m Rapid Fire Pistol, and IPSC practical shooting. Pistols are designed for accuracy and speed, with ergonomic grips, adjustable sights, and lightweight frames that facilitate quick aiming and shooting.

- **Shotguns:** Essential for dynamic shooting sports like trap, skeet, and sporting clays. Shotguns are designed to hit moving targets, with features like interchangeable chokes, smooth actions, and reliable firing mechanisms that accommodate rapid shots in quick succession.

Choosing the Right Firearm:

- **Fit and Comfort:** The firearm should fit comfortably and be easy to handle. Factors like stock length, weight, and grip size play a crucial role in shooter comfort and control.
- **Purpose:** Select a firearm based on the specific shooting discipline. For example, precision shooting requires rifles with high magnification scopes, while practical shooting favors lightweight pistols with rapid-fire capabilities.
- **Quality and Brand:** Invest in high-quality firearms from reputable manufacturers. Reliability, durability, and ease of maintenance are critical factors to consider.

2. Ammunition

Purpose and Importance

Ammunition selection is crucial for achieving optimal performance in shooting sports. The type, quality, and consistency of ammunition can greatly influence accuracy, range, and overall results.

Types of Ammunition:

- **Rifle Ammunition:** Includes .22 caliber for small-bore events and larger calibers for high-power rifle

competitions. Match-grade ammunition offers precise manufacturing tolerances for consistent performance.
- **Pistol Ammunition:** Typically ranges from .177 caliber pellets for air pistols to larger calibers like 9mm for practical shooting. Consistent velocity and minimal recoil are key considerations.
- **Shotgun Shells:** Used in trap, skeet, and sporting clays, with variations in shot size and load tailored to the target type. Shotgun shells are available in multiple gauges, with 12-gauge being the most common in competitions.

Choosing the Right Ammunition:

- **Compatibility:** Ensure that the ammunition is compatible with your firearm and meets the specifications for the shooting discipline.
- **Quality:** Opt for high-quality, consistent ammunition from trusted brands. Match-grade options are ideal for competition, while standard rounds may suffice for training.
- **Purpose:** Select ammunition that suits the intended use, such as lighter loads for practice or premium rounds for competition to minimize variability in performance.

3. Protective Gear

Purpose and Importance

Protective gear is essential for safeguarding shooters from potential hazards such as noise, recoil, and accidental discharges. Proper protection enhances comfort and concentration, allowing shooters to focus on performance.

Types of Protective Gear:

- **Eye Protection:** Shooting glasses are mandatory in most disciplines to protect against flying debris, shell casings, and potential accidents. They come in various lens colors for different lighting conditions and enhance contrast for better target visibility.
- **Ear Protection:** Essential for reducing the harmful noise levels generated by firearms. Options include earplugs and earmuffs, with electronic versions offering adjustable sound amplification for hearing range commands while blocking out gunfire noise.
- **Shooting Jackets and Gloves:** Worn primarily in rifle and pistol disciplines to provide stability and reduce muscle fatigue. Shooting jackets offer padded support for the shoulders and elbows, while gloves enhance grip and control.

Choosing Protective Gear

- **Fit and Comfort:** Protective gear should fit securely without restricting movement. Ensure that ear and eye protection do not interfere with the firearm's operation or your shooting stance.
- **Quality:** Invest in gear that meets safety standards and provides adequate protection. Look for features like anti-fog coatings on glasses and noise reduction ratings (NRR) for ear protection.

4. Scopes and Sights

Purpose and Importance

Scopes and sights are vital for aiming precision, providing visual enhancements that help shooters align their shots accurately. The right optics can significantly improve a shooter's accuracy, particularly in disciplines that involve long-range targets or rapid target transitions.

Types of Scopes and Sights:

- **Telescopic Scopes:** Commonly used in rifle events, telescopic scopes offer magnification to help shooters see distant targets clearly. They feature adjustable reticles, parallax settings, and turrets for windage and elevation adjustments.
- **Red Dot Sights:** Popular in practical shooting and pistol events, red dot sights provide a clear aiming point without magnification, allowing for quick target acquisition and precise shooting at closer ranges.
- **Iron Sights:** Traditional sights used in many shooting disciplines, consisting of a front post and rear notch or aperture. Iron sights require precise alignment but offer reliability and simplicity.

Choosing Scopes and Sights:

- **Magnification Needs:** Select a scope with appropriate magnification for the shooting distance. Lower magnification is suitable for close-range and rapid shooting, while higher magnification is needed for long-distance precision.

- **Durability:** Ensure that the optics are durable, shockproof, and weather-resistant to handle the rigors of competition and outdoor conditions.
- **Compatibility:** Match the scope or sight to your firearm and intended discipline, ensuring proper mounting and zeroing.

5. Range Bags and Tool Kits

Purpose and Importance

Range bags and tool kits keep essential equipment organized and readily accessible, making them indispensable for both training and competition. A well-equipped range bag allows shooters to carry firearms, ammunition, protective gear, and maintenance tools efficiently.

Components of a Range Bag

- **Storage Compartments:** Range bags feature multiple compartments for securely storing firearms, ammunition, and accessories. Look for padded sections to protect delicate items like optics.
- **Maintenance Tools:** A basic tool kit should include cleaning rods, brushes, oil, patches, and multitools for on-the-spot firearm maintenance and repairs.
- **Shooting Accessories:** Include items like extra magazines, spare earplugs, targets, and shooting logs for recording performance and adjustments.

Choosing a Range Bag

- **Size and Capacity:** Choose a bag that accommodates all your gear without being too bulky or cumbersome.

The size should match your specific needs, from basic shooting sessions to extended competition setups.
- **Durability:** Look for bags made from durable materials with reinforced stitching, heavy-duty zippers, and water-resistant coatings to withstand regular use and outdoor conditions.

6. Maintenance and Cleaning Supplies

Purpose and Importance

Regular maintenance is crucial for ensuring the longevity, safety, and performance of firearms. Cleaning supplies help remove fouling, prevent corrosion, and keep mechanisms operating smoothly, reducing the risk of malfunctions during use.

Essential Cleaning Supplies

- **Cleaning Rods and Brushes:** Used to clean the bore of the firearm, removing residue and debris that can affect accuracy. Brushes should match the caliber of the firearm for effective cleaning.
- **Solvents and Oils:** Solvents dissolve carbon buildup and fouling, while oils lubricate moving parts to reduce wear and corrosion. Choose non-toxic, firearm-specific products for best results.
- **Patches and Cloths:** Use patches to apply solvents and oils, and microfiber cloths for wiping down and polishing the exterior of the firearm.

Maintaining Your Firearm:

- **Regular Cleaning:** Clean your firearm after each use, paying attention to the bore, chamber, and moving parts. Regular maintenance prevents buildup that can impede function and accuracy.
- **Inspection:** Routinely inspect your firearm for signs of wear, damage, or loose components. Address any issues promptly to ensure safe and reliable operation.

7. Choosing the Right Gear for You:

Selecting the appropriate shooting gear is essential for both safety and performance. Here are some tips for choosing the best equipment:

Firearms:

- **Purpose:** Determine the primary use of the firearm (competition, training, or hunting) to select the appropriate type and features.
- **Fit:** Test different models to find the best fit and balance for your body type and shooting style.
- **Brand and Quality:** Invest in reputable brands known for reliability and precision. Seek recommendations from experienced shooters and read reviews.

Ammunition

- **Quality:** Use match-grade or high-quality ammunition for competition to ensure consistency and accuracy.
- **Compatibility:** Verify that the ammunition matches your firearm's specifications and the requirements of the shooting discipline.

Protective Gear

- **Fit and Comfort:** Try on protective gear to ensure a secure and comfortable fit that does not interfere with shooting.
- **Safety Standards:** Choose gear that meets industry safety standards for maximum protection.

Range Bags and Tool Kits:

- **Organization:** Opt for a range bag with ample compartments and easy access to essential items.
- **Quality:** Durable materials and reinforced construction are crucial for longevity and protecting your gear.

Maintenance Supplies:

- **Regular Use:** Keep a well-stocked cleaning kit for routine maintenance to prevent malfunctions and extend the life of your firearms.
- **Proper Storage:** Store cleaning supplies in a cool, dry place to preserve their effectiveness.

Proper care and maintenance of your shooting gear not only ensure its longevity but also enhance safety and performance. By investing in high-quality equipment and adhering to these maintenance tips, you'll be well-prepared for both training and competition, ensuring a rewarding and safe experience in the world of shooting sports.

4

SHOOTING STANCE AND MOVEMENT

SHOOTING SPORTS ARE ABOUT MORE THAN JUST pulling the trigger; they require a blend of precision, strategy, and movement. Central to mastering any shooting discipline is understanding the importance of a solid stance and effective movement. This chapter provides an extensive guide to shooting stances, their significance, and detailed movement techniques that are essential for both static and dynamic shooting sports.

THE IMPORTANCE OF A SOLID STANCE

Stamp of India—Beijing 2008 Olympics

A shooter's stance is the foundation of their stability, accuracy, and overall performance. A proper stance not only supports shooting precision but also influences the ability to manage recoil, move effectively, and maintain endurance during extended sessions. Here's a closer look at why a solid stance is essential:

The great pigeon shooting match, Greenville, New Jersey
(wood engraving with letterpress)

- **Stability and Balance:** A well-established stance ensures that the shooter remains balanced and stable, even when shooting from challenging positions or under pressure. The stance distributes weight evenly, allowing the shooter to maintain a low center of gravity and manage the firearm's recoil effectively. Stability is critical in maintaining the sight alignment and sight picture, which directly impacts shot accuracy.
- **Accuracy and Consistency:** A consistent stance helps shooters develop muscle memory, allowing for more precise shots. By anchoring the body in a reliable position, shooters can focus on fine motor skills, such as trigger control, rather than compensating for imbalance or movement.
- **Recoil Management:** Proper stance and body positioning are crucial for managing recoil, especially in high-caliber rifles and shotguns. By positioning the body to absorb and control recoil, shooters can quickly

return to target, making follow-up shots more efficient.
- **Endurance and Comfort:** In shooting sports, especially in competitive or long-duration scenarios, maintaining a comfortable and sustainable stance is vital. A proper stance reduces fatigue, allowing the shooter to perform consistently over time.

BASIC SHOOTING STANCES: ISOSCELES VS. WEAVER VS. MODIFIED STANCES

In shooting sports, there are several fundamental stances, each with its own unique advantages and suitable applications depending on the type of shooting, the firearm used, and personal preference.

DF Shooting Competition 2010

ISOSCELES STANCE

- **Description:** Named for its resemblance to an isosceles triangle, this stance involves positioning the feet shoulder-width apart, with both arms extended straight towards the target. The shooter's body faces the target squarely, with knees slightly bent for flexibility and balance.
- **Advantages:**
  - *Symmetry and Simplicity:* This stance provides a straightforward approach, with a symmetrical arm and body positioning that simplifies aiming and recoil management.
  - *Recoil Absorption:* The squared stance and extended arms help distribute recoil forces evenly across the body, enhancing stability and control.
  - *Field of Vision:* Facing the target directly maximizes the shooter's peripheral vision, making it easier to spot additional targets or changes in the environment.
- **Applications:** Commonly used in pistol shooting, the isosceles stance is favored in sports like IPSC and IDPA for its simplicity and ease of use under pressure.

WEAVER STANCE

- **Description:** The Weaver stance involves positioning the body at a slight angle to the target, with the feet shoulder-width apart. The dominant foot is placed slightly back, and the knees are bent. The arms are extended, but the dominant arm is pushed out more,

creating tension between the push of the dominant arm and the pull of the support arm.
- **Advantages:**
  - *Recoil Management:* The tension created by the push-pull dynamic helps manage recoil, making it easier to maintain sight alignment and return to target quickly.
  - *Natural Point of Aim:* This stance allows for a more natural point of aim, particularly beneficial when shooting rapidly or moving between targets.
  - *Versatility:* The angled body position makes the Weaver stance adaptable for dynamic shooting, where movement and quick target transitions are required.
- **Applications:** Often used in competitive shooting and self-defense scenarios, the Weaver stance is popular among shooters who prefer a more dynamic approach to recoil management.

MODIFIED STANCES

- **Description:** Modified stances, such as the Modified Weaver or Modified Isosceles, blend elements of the basic stances to suit individual shooter preferences or specific shooting conditions. These stances adjust body positioning, arm extension, or foot placement to improve comfort, recoil management, or shooting accuracy.
- **Advantages:**
  - *Customization:* Modified stances allow shooters to tailor their stance to their body type, firearm, and shooting style, enhancing overall performance.

- - *Adaptability:* These stances are particularly useful in dynamic shooting environments, where the shooter may need to adjust positioning quickly to maintain effectiveness.
  - *Recoil and Comfort Balance:* By customizing the stance, shooters can find an optimal balance between recoil control and comfort, especially important during extended shooting sessions.
- **Applications:** Modified stances are widely used across various shooting sports, including 3-gun competitions, tactical shooting, and hunting scenarios, where versatility and adaptability are key.

MOVEMENT TECHNIQUES: ADVANCING, RETREATING, AND LATERAL MOVEMENT

Effective movement is crucial in many shooting disciplines, allowing the shooter to maintain control, adjust positioning, and engage multiple targets. Mastering these movement fundamentals can greatly enhance a shooter's tactical advantage and performance.

Advancing (Moving Forward)

- **Purpose:** Advancing towards the target is essential for closing the distance in tactical or competition scenarios. This movement enables shooters to engage targets more effectively, especially in environments with limited visibility or obstacles.
- **Technique:**
  - *Step with the Lead Foot:* Begin by stepping forward with the lead foot, ensuring that the movement is

deliberate and controlled. The lead foot should point towards the target, with the knee slightly bent for flexibility.
  - *Follow with the Rear Foot:* As the lead foot steps forward, the rear foot follows, maintaining the proper stance width. This ensures that the shooter remains balanced and prepared to engage targets.
  - *Maintain Sight Alignment:* Throughout the movement, focus on keeping the firearm aimed at the target, with minimal disruption to sight alignment. Smooth, controlled steps are crucial for maintaining accuracy.
- **Drills:** Practice advancing by moving forward in a straight line towards a target while maintaining a proper stance and sight picture. Gradually increase speed while focusing on balance and accuracy.

Retreating (Moving Backward)

- **Purpose:** Retreating is used to create distance from a threat or to reposition to a more advantageous location. This movement helps shooters avoid incoming threats while maintaining control over the shooting environment.
- **Technique:**
  - *Step Back with the Rear Foot:* Begin the retreat by stepping backwards with the rear foot, ensuring that the movement is smooth and balanced. The step should be deliberate, with the foot landing securely.
  - *Follow with the Lead Foot:* As the rear foot moves back, the lead foot follows, maintaining the proper

stance and alignment. This ensures that the shooter remains balanced and capable of engaging targets while retreating.
  - *Keep the Upper Body Stable:* Focus on minimizing upper body movement to maintain a steady aim on the target. A stable upper body is crucial for accurate shooting while in motion.
- **Drills:** Practice retreating by moving backwards from a target, focusing on smooth, controlled steps and maintaining sight alignment. Incorporate varying speeds and distances to simulate different retreat scenarios.

Lateral Movement (Side-to-Side)

- **Purpose:** Lateral movement is essential for maneuvering around obstacles, adjusting angles of engagement, and avoiding potential threats. This movement allows shooters to maintain control of the shooting environment and exploit advantageous positions.
- **Technique:**
  - *Step with the Lead Foot:* Begin by stepping laterally with the lead foot, moving in the desired direction. Keep the step short and controlled to maintain balance.
  - *Follow with the Rear Foot:* As the lead foot moves, the rear foot follows, maintaining stance width and balance. This ensures that the shooter remains stable and prepared to engage targets from different angles.
  - *Minimize Upper Body Movement:* Focus on keeping the upper body stable to maintain sight alignment. Avoid unnecessary swaying or bobbing, which can disrupt aim.

- **Drills:** Practice lateral movement by moving side-to-side along a shooting line, engaging targets from various angles. Incorporate barriers or obstacles to simulate real-world scenarios and improve adaptability.

DRILLS TO IMPROVE STANCE AND MOVEMENT

Incorporating specific drills into training routines can significantly enhance a shooter's stance, balance, and movement capabilities. Here's an extensive guide to some of the most effective drills for mastering stance and movement in shooting sports:

Dry-Fire Movement Drills

- **Purpose:** Dry-fire drills allow shooters to practice stance and movement without live ammunition, focusing on form, balance, and sight alignment.
- **Drill:**
  - *Start in Stance:* Begin in your chosen stance and practice moving forward, backwards, and laterally without live firing. Focus on maintaining a stable stance and smooth movements.
  - *Incorporate Firearm Presentation:* Practice drawing and presenting the firearm while moving, ensuring that the movement does not disrupt sight alignment.
  - *Focus on Transitions:* Work on transitioning between different movements (e.g., from advancing to retreating) smoothly, maintaining control and balance throughout.
- **Benefits:** Dry-fire movement drills help shooters refine their stance and movement techniques without the

added stress of live fire. They are ideal for reinforcing fundamentals and developing muscle memory.

Shooting on the Move

- **Purpose:** Shooting on-the-move drills combine movement with live fire, challenging shooters to maintain accuracy while advancing, retreating, or moving laterally.
- **Drill:**
  - *Set Up Targets:* Place multiple targets at varying distances and angles. Practice moving between targets while maintaining stance and shooting accuracy.
  - *Vary Speeds and Directions:* Adjust the speed of movement and the direction (forward, backwards, lateral) to simulate different scenarios. Focus on maintaining a stable shooting platform throughout.
  - *Evaluate Performance:* Assess the accuracy and consistency of shots while moving. Identify areas for improvement, such as balance or recoil management.
- **Benefits:** Shooting on the move drills help shooters develop confidence and competence in dynamic shooting scenarios, essential for competitive and tactical environments.

Obstacle Navigation

- **Purpose:** Obstacle navigation drills simulate real-world scenarios where shooters must move around barriers, through doorways, or over uneven terrain while maintaining shooting accuracy.
- **Drill:**
  - *Set Up Obstacles:* Arrange barriers, cones, or

other obstacles in a shooting lane. Practice moving through the obstacles while engaging targets.
- *Focus on Stance Adjustments:* As you navigate obstacles, adjust your stance as needed to maintain balance and control. Practice shooting from unconventional positions if required.
- *Incorporate Time Pressure:* Add a timer to the drill to introduce time pressure, simulating competitive or tactical scenarios. Focus on maintaining composure and control under stress.
- **Benefits:** Obstacle navigation drills build agility, adaptability, and confidence in handling complex shooting environments. They are particularly useful for competitive shooters and those in tactical disciplines.

Buddy Movement Drills

- **Purpose:** Buddy movement drills involve practicing movement and shooting with a partner, emphasizing communication, coordination, and mutual support.
- **Drill:**
    - *Paired Movement:* Work in pairs, with one shooter moving while the other covers. Practice advancing, retreating, and moving laterally in coordination.
    - *Communicate Effectively:* Use verbal and non-verbal cues to coordinate movement and shooting. Focus on maintaining clear communication to enhance safety and effectiveness.
    - *Evaluate Coordination:* Assess how well you and your partner coordinate movement and shooting. Identify areas for improvement, such as timing or communication.

SHOOTING STANCE AND MOVEMENT

- **Benefits:** Buddy movement drills enhance teamwork and communication skills, crucial for scenarios where shooters must work together, such as in tactical operations or team-based competitions.

Welsh 50 meter open shooting competition in Tondu

Mastering stance and movement is a fundamental component of success in shooting sports. A solid stance provides the foundation for balance, control, and accuracy, while effective movement techniques enable shooters to navigate dynamic environments with confidence. By understanding and practicing the various stances, footwork, and movement drills outlined in this chapter, shooters can develop a robust foundation that supports both precision and adaptability in the field. Consistent practice, attention to detail, and a commitment to refining these skills will lead to enhanced performance in both competitive and practical shooting contexts.

SECTION TWO

THE BASICS

5

BASIC SHOOTING TECHNIQUES AND COMBINATIONS

IN SHOOTING SPORTS, MASTERING THE FUNDAMENTAL shooting techniques and target engagement strategies is essential for developing a well-rounded skill set. This chapter covers the basic shooting techniques—stance, grip, sight alignment, trigger control, and follow-through—as well as how to combine these elements effectively. Understanding these fundamentals will help you build a solid foundation for accuracy, consistency, and confidence in various shooting disciplines.

THE STANCE: THE FOUNDATION OF ACCURACY

The stance is often referred to as the foundation of shooting. It provides stability, balance, and support, which are critical for accurate shooting. Here's why the stance is so crucial:

- **Stability and Balance:** A proper stance ensures that the shooter remains balanced, even during recoil. This

BASIC SHOOTING TECHNIQUES AND COMBINATIONS

stability is achieved through proper weight distribution between both feet and maintaining a low center of gravity, allowing the shooter to handle recoil effectively and return to the target quickly.

- **Consistency:** A consistent stance helps shooters develop muscle memory, enabling them to replicate the same position each time they shoot. This consistency is key to achieving tight shot groupings and improving overall accuracy.
- **Recoil Management:** The stance plays a significant role in managing recoil, particularly in rapid-fire situations. By positioning the feet and body correctly, shooters can absorb and control the firearm's backward force, making follow-up shots faster and more accurate.

Anonymous engraving of a national shooting contest medal in Sweden, designed by Julius Husborg, Aftonbladet, 1903

- **Endurance:** A good stance is also about comfort and sustainability. During long shooting sessions or competitions, maintaining a comfortable stance reduces fatigue and helps maintain shooting accuracy over time.

Technique:

1. **Starting Position:** Stand with your feet shoulder-width apart, with your non-dominant foot slightly forward. Your weight should be evenly distributed between both feet, and your knees should be slightly bent.

2. **Lean Forward:** Slightly lean your upper body forward, shifting your weight towards your toes. This helps in managing recoil and maintaining balance.
3. **Align Your Shoulders:** Keep your shoulders squared to the target and relaxed. Your arms should be extended but not locked, allowing for fluid movement and control.
4. **Maintain Head Position:** Keep your head upright and aligned with your sight. Avoid tilting your head or shifting your focus away from the target.

Grip: Controlling the Firearm

The grip is another fundamental element of shooting. A proper grip ensures control over the firearm, affects recoil management, and directly influences accuracy. Here's how to perfect your grip:

- **Control and Stability:** A firm, consistent grip provides control over the firearm during recoil, helping to keep the sights aligned for follow-up shots. It also minimizes movement, which can cause shots to stray off target.
- **Consistency:** Like the stance, a consistent grip is essential for accurate shooting. The grip should be firm but not so tight that it causes tension in the hands or arms. A proper grip allows for repeatability, making each shot feel the same.
- **Recoil Management:** A good grip helps manage recoil by distributing the forces across the shooter's hands and arms. This control allows the shooter to quickly realign the sights after each shot, essential for rapid-fire scenarios.

Technique:

1. **Hand Placement:** For pistols, place your dominant hand high on the backstrap of the gun, with your fingers wrapped around the grip. Your thumb should rest along the frame, pointing towards the target.
2. **Support Hand:** Use your support hand to wrap around the dominant hand, with fingers interlaced or layered. The support hand should apply pressure from the side, enhancing grip strength and control.
3. **Thumb Position:** Both thumbs should point forward towards the target, aligning with the barrel of the gun. This positioning aids in natural pointing and stability.
4. **Grip Pressure:** Apply firm but even pressure with both hands. Avoid gripping too tightly, which can cause shaking or tension. The grip should feel natural and secure.

SIGHT ALIGNMENT AND SIGHT PICTURE

Sight alignment and sight picture are critical components of aiming. Properly aligning the sights ensures that the shooter's point of aim is consistent with the intended point of impact.

- **Sight Alignment:** This involves lining up the front sight post with the rear sight notch, ensuring that the top of the front sight is level with the top of the rear sight and centered within the notch.
- **Sight Picture:** This is the visual relationship between the aligned sights and the target. The front sight should be sharp and clear, with the target slightly blurred in

the background. This focus ensures that the point of impact matches the point of aim.

Technique:

1. **Focus on the Front Sight:** Keep your eyes focused on the front sight while aligning it with the rear sight. The target should appear slightly out of focus, with the front sight sharp and clear.
2. **Align Horizontally and Vertically:** Ensure that the front sight is centered within the rear sight notch and level at the top. This alignment prevents shots from veering off to the side or above/below the intended target.
3. **Maintain Consistency:** Consistent sight alignment is key to accurate shooting. Practice aligning the sights quickly and accurately, especially during rapid shooting sequences.

Trigger Control: The Key to Precision

Trigger control is arguably the most critical aspect of shooting, as improper trigger manipulation can lead to missed shots even with perfect stance and sight alignment.

- **Smooth Press:** A smooth, controlled press of the trigger is essential for maintaining sight alignment during the shot. Jerking or slapping the trigger can cause the sights to move off target, resulting in inaccurate shots.
- **Reset Control:** Understanding trigger reset—where the trigger moves just far enough forward to re-engage the sear—is crucial for rapid shooting. Learning to feel the reset point allows shooters to minimize unnecessary trigger movement, improving shot-to-shot consistency.

Technique:

1. **Finger Placement:** Place the pad of your trigger finger on the trigger, avoiding excessive contact with the finger joint. This positioning allows for a straight-back pull, minimizing lateral movement.
2. **Slow, Steady Press:** Apply gradual, even pressure to the trigger until the shot breaks. Avoid jerking or anticipating the recoil; the goal is a surprise break.
3. **Follow Through:** After the shot, continue to hold the trigger back momentarily, then slowly release to the reset point. This follow-through helps maintain control and prepares for the next shot.

Follow-Through: Completing the Shot

Follow-through is the act of maintaining the shooting fundamentals (stance, grip, sight picture, and trigger control) after the shot is fired. Proper follow-through ensures that any movements or adjustments needed are minimal, enhancing overall accuracy.

- **Recoil Management:** By maintaining stance and grip during follow-through, shooters can better manage recoil and prepare for follow-up shots.
- **Consistency:** Consistent follow-through helps reinforce muscle memory and makes the shooting process more uniform from shot to shot.

Technique:

1. **Maintain Sight Picture:** After the shot, keep your sights aligned on the target. This practice helps in assessing

the shot placement and preparing for any needed adjustments.
2. **Control Recoil:** Use your stance and grip to absorb recoil without losing sight alignment. This control is essential for quick target reacquisition.
3. **Reset and Reassess:** Allow the trigger to reset while maintaining your shooting fundamentals. Reassess your sight picture and make the necessary corrections before taking the next shot.

BASIC SHOOTING COMBINATIONS AND THEIR USES

Combining the basic shooting techniques allows shooters to engage targets efficiently and effectively. Here's a guide to some fundamental shooting combinations and their applications:

Controlled Pair

- **Purpose:** A controlled pair, or double-tap, involves two quick but accurate shots at the same target. This combination is used to ensure that the target is neutralized or to maximize scoring in competitions.
- **Application:** Engage the target with a smooth trigger press, follow through, and immediately reset for a second shot. Maintain stance and sight picture throughout the sequence for consistency and accuracy.

Transition Shots

- **Purpose:** Transition shots involve engaging multiple targets in succession. This combination tests the

shooter's ability to maintain fundamentals while shifting focus between different points of aim.
- **Application:** After engaging the first target, smoothly transition to the next by shifting your upper body and eyes, then realigning your sights. Maintain a stable stance and grip throughout the transitions to ensure accuracy.

Hammer Pair

- **Purpose:** A hammer pair consists of two rapid shots fired with minimal trigger reset. This technique is used when speed is essential, such as in close-quarters shooting or timed competitions.
- **Application:** Engage the target with two rapid shots, focusing on maintaining control and sight alignment. Practice minimizing the trigger reset between shots for maximum speed and efficiency.

Shoot and Move

- **Purpose:** This combination involves shooting while moving, a critical skill in dynamic shooting sports and tactical scenarios. The objective is to maintain accuracy while adjusting positions to avoid threats or gain a tactical advantage.
- **Application:** Practice engaging targets while advancing, retreating, or moving laterally. Focus on maintaining a stable shooting platform and sight alignment despite the movement.

Shooting ranges, London 2012

DRILLS TO PRACTICE BASIC TECHNIQUES AND COMBINATIONS

Dry Fire Practice

- **Purpose:** Dry fire practice allows shooters to refine their stance, grip, sight alignment, and trigger control without live ammunition. This practice reinforces muscle memory and improves technique.
- **Drill:**
  - *Routine Practice:* Set up a target (or use a blank wall) and practice going through the shooting motions—stance, grip, sight alignment, trigger press, and follow-through—without a live fire.
  - *Repetition:* Repeat the sequence multiple times, focusing on consistency and smoothness of motion.

- *Assessment:* Use a mirror or video to assess the form and make adjustments as needed.

Target Transitions

- **Purpose:** Target transition drills enhance the ability to engage multiple targets accurately and efficiently. This drill builds confidence and skill in shifting focus between different points of aim.
- **Drill:**
  - *Set Up Multiple Targets:* Arrange targets at varying distances and angles. Practice transitioning between targets smoothly, maintaining fundamentals throughout.
  - *Vary Speed:* Start at a comfortable speed and gradually increase as accuracy improves. Focus on keeping sight alignment and trigger control consistent.
  - *Evaluate Performance:* Assess shot groupings and transitions to identify areas for improvement.

Controlled Pair Drills

- **Purpose:** Controlled pair drills focus on delivering two accurate shots in quick succession. This drill improves speed and recoil management while maintaining accuracy.
- **Drill:**
  - *Engage with Pairs:* Practice engaging a single target with two shots, focusing on sight alignment and smooth trigger press for each shot.
  - *Adjust Timing:* Vary the timing between shots to find the optimal balance between speed and accuracy.

- *Consistency Check:* Ensure that both shots land in the intended target area, adjusting as necessary to improve control.

Movement Drills

- **Purpose:** Movement drills combine shooting with physical movements, such as advancing, retreating, or moving laterally. These drills improve the shooter's ability to maintain fundamentals while on the move.
- **Drill:**
  - *Incorporate Movement:* Set up a course or shooting line and practice moving while engaging targets. Focus on maintaining stance and sight alignment during movement.
  - *Simulate Scenarios:* Create scenarios that require different types of movement, such as navigating obstacles or engaging targets from unconventional positions.
  - *Evaluate Adaptability:* Assess how well the shooter maintains accuracy and control while moving. Identify areas for improvement, such as balance or recoil management.

Recoil Management

- **Purpose:** Recoil management drills help shooters control recoil and maintain sight alignment for quick follow-up shots. These drills are essential for improving overall shooting speed and accuracy.
- **Drill:**
  - *Rapid Fire Sequences:* Practice shooting rapid sequences, focusing on controlling recoil and

realigning sights after each shot.
- *Adjust Stance and Grip:* Experiment with different stances and grips to find the most effective combination for recoil management.
- *Consistency Check:* Evaluate how quickly and accurately the shooter can return to target after each shot.

Women's target shooting – Dene – Great Slave Lake NWT c1940

A boy shoots at an electronic target board
(Operation Ice, 2023). Tyumen, Russia

6

DEFENSIVE TECHNIQUES IN SHOOTING SPORTS

IN SHOOTING SPORTS, DEFENSE ISN'T ABOUT protecting yourself from physical attacks, but rather ensuring safety, stability, and precision in various competitive and practical scenarios. Effective defensive techniques include understanding recoil management, handling malfunctions, shooting from unconventional positions, and developing situational awareness. Mastering these techniques will enhance your shooting skills, improve your overall effectiveness, and ensure you remain safe under pressure.

RECOIL MANAGEMENT

Recoil management is a fundamental defensive technique in shooting sports. It involves controlling the firearm's backward force when a shot is fired, which is crucial for maintaining accuracy and ensuring quick follow-up shots.

DEFENSIVE TECHNIQUES IN SHOOTING SPORTS

Undated Bain News Service image of exhibition shooter Elizabeth 'Mrs. Adolph' Topperwein

- **Purpose:** Proper recoil management helps keep the firearm stable during and after firing, allowing the shooter to quickly reacquire the target and fire successive shots accurately. This is essential in both competitive settings, where speed and precision are key, and in tactical scenarios, where control under stress is vital.
- **Technique:**
  - *Grip and Stance:* Use a firm grip and stable stance to absorb and control recoil. Ensure your grip is consistent, with the dominant hand high on the backstrap and the support hand wrapped around firmly.

- *Lean Into the Shot:* Slightly lean forward with your upper body, distributing your weight towards your toes. This position helps absorb the backward force and prevents the firearm from pushing you off balance.
- *Follow-Through:* Maintain focus on the sights and follow through after each shot. Allow the firearm to return to its original position naturally, and avoid fighting the recoil with excessive force.

Clay shooting with a semi-auto shotgun

- **Drills:**
  - *Controlled Pair Drills:* Practice firing two quick shots in succession, focusing on maintaining control and minimizing muzzle rise between shots. Start slowly and increase speed as you maintain accuracy.
  - *Recoil Tracking Drills:* Use a laser sight or dummy rounds to practice tracking the firearm's movement

during dry fire. Focus on keeping the sight aligned with the target throughout the shot cycle.

MALFUNCTION HANDLING

Malfunction handling involves quickly diagnosing and clearing firearm malfunctions, which is essential for maintaining safety and continuity in shooting. Common malfunctions include misfires, stovepipes, and double feeds.

- **Purpose:** Efficiently clearing malfunctions prevents disruptions during shooting and ensures that the firearm remains operational. This skill is critical in both competition and defensive scenarios, where a malfunction could have serious consequences.
- **Technique:**
  - *Immediate Action Drill:* If a malfunction occurs, tap the magazine to ensure it is seated properly, rack the slide to clear the malfunction, and assess if the firearm is ready to fire.
  - *Identify the Malfunction:* Learn to identify common malfunctions by feel and visual inspection. For example, a stovepipe (a shell casing stuck in the ejection port) requires a quick rack of the slide, while a double feed may require locking the slide back, removing the magazine, and clearing the chamber.
  - *Practice Under Stress:* Simulate malfunctions during practice to build muscle memory. The goal is to develop the ability to clear malfunctions without hesitation, maintaining focus on the target and environment.

- **Drills:**
  - *Malfunction Clearance Drills:* Set up malfunctions intentionally using dummy rounds or snap caps. Practice clearing these malfunctions rapidly, focusing on proper technique and maintaining safety.
  - *Timed Malfunction Drills:* Add a timer to your malfunction clearance drills to introduce time pressure, simulating real-world stress conditions. Track your progress in reducing the time needed to clear malfunctions accurately.

Goodwin & Company: Pigeon Shooting (1889)

SHOOTING FROM UNCONVENTIONAL POSITIONS

Shooting from unconventional positions is an advanced defensive technique that involves engaging targets from atypical stances, such as prone, kneeling, or from behind cover. This skill is crucial in dynamic shooting environments where standard stances may not be possible.

DEFENSIVE TECHNIQUES IN SHOOTING SPORTS

- **Purpose:** Shooting from unconventional positions enhances versatility and adaptability, allowing shooters to maintain accuracy and control regardless of the circumstances. This is particularly important in practical shooting scenarios, where obstacles or tactical considerations may require non-standard positioning.
- **Technique:**
  - *Prone Position:* Lie flat on your stomach with your legs spread for stability. Use your elbows to support the firearm and maintain sight alignment. This position provides a low profile and a stable shooting platform.
  - *Kneeling Position:* Drop to one knee, using your supporting arm to brace against your forward knee. This position is quick to assume and provides moderate stability, making it ideal for shooting from cover.
  - *Shooting from Cover:* Use cover effectively by exposing as little of your body as possible. Keep your firearm close to cover but avoid resting it directly against the cover to prevent interference with recoil management.
- **Drills:**
  - *Position Transition Drills:* Practice transitioning between different shooting positions (standing to kneeling, kneeling to prone) while maintaining sight alignment and control.

45th World Shooting Championships, Moscow. Competitors and Target (5 June 1990)

Focus on fluid movements and minimizing exposure.
- *Barricade Drills:* Use simulated cover such as barricades or walls. Practice shooting from around, over, and under cover, focusing on maintaining accuracy and minimizing your exposure to threats.

DEFENSIVE RELOADING TECHNIQUES

Defensive reloading involves efficiently reloading your firearm under pressure, ensuring that you can continue shooting with minimal downtime. This skill is crucial in scenarios where extended shooting or a high rate of fire is required.

- **Purpose:** Proper reloading techniques allow shooters to maintain operational readiness and avoid being caught with an empty firearm. Quick and smooth reloads are essential for maintaining momentum in competition and tactical situations.
- **Technique:**
  - *Emergency Reloads:* When the firearm runs empty, quickly drop the empty magazine while reaching for a fresh one. Insert the new magazine firmly, then release the slide to chamber a round. This method is fast but can be less controlled if not practiced extensively.
  - *Tactical Reloads:* Conduct a tactical reload when there is a lull in shooting, and there are still rounds left in the magazine. Swap the partially used magazine with a full one, retaining the partially used magazine for later use.

DEFENSIVE TECHNIQUES IN SHOOTING SPORTS

- *Speed vs. Control:* Focus on both speed and control, ensuring that the reload is executed smoothly without fumbling. Proper magazine handling and a consistent reloading motion are key.
- **Drills:**
  - *Emergency Reload Drills:* Practice emergency reloads under time pressure, using both dry fire and live fire exercises. Focus on minimizing the time taken to reload while maintaining safety and control.
  - *Tactical Reload Drills:* Practice tactical reloads during movement or while transitioning between shooting positions. The goal is to develop fluidity and minimize downtime while keeping your firearm ready.

MANAGING MULTIPLE TARGETS

Engaging multiple targets is a defensive technique that involves quickly and accurately transitioning between multiple points of aim. This skill is essential in both competitive and tactical scenarios, where shooters must handle various threats simultaneously.

- **Purpose:** Managing multiple targets effectively enhances a shooter's ability to handle complex shooting scenarios, improving situational adaptability and control.
- **Technique:**
  - *Target Priority:* Determine the order in which to engage targets based on the threat level, proximity, or other criteria. This decision-making process is crucial for maintaining control and safety.

- *Smooth Transitions:* Use smooth, controlled movements to transition between targets. Avoid jerky or exaggerated motions, which can cause the sights to stray off target.
- *Follow Through:* After engaging each target, maintain follow-through by keeping your sights aligned and ready for any necessary follow-up shots.
- **Drills:**
  - *Transition Drills:* Set up multiple targets at varying distances and angles. Practice engaging them in sequence, focusing on smooth transitions, and maintaining sight alignment throughout.
  - *Timed Multiple Target Drills:* Add a timer to your multiple target drills to introduce time pressure. This helps simulate competitive or defensive shooting conditions, improving both speed and accuracy.

Defensive techniques are essential for any successful shooter, whether in competitive sports, tactical scenarios, or recreational activities. Mastering recoil management, handling malfunctions, shooting from unconventional positions, maintaining situational awareness, defensive reloading, and managing multiple targets will significantly enhance your shooting skills and overall performance. Consistent practice and application of these techniques in training will help you remain safe, adaptable, and effective, allowing you to handle any shooting scenario with confidence. As you develop your defensive skills, remember that a strong foundation in these basics is the key to excelling in shooting sports and beyond.

Dallinger during the final of the World Cup

The skills you develop will not only make you a better shooter but will also contribute to your growth as a disciplined, focused, and resilient individual. Whether on the range or in everyday life, the principles you learn through shooting sports will serve you well, helping you to navigate challenges with confidence and precision.

In conclusion, defensive techniques in shooting sports are not merely about achieving accuracy under pressure; they encompass a broader set of skills that promote safety, discipline, and personal growth. By committing to regular practice and continuously challenging yourself, you will not only excel in shooting sports but also cultivate qualities that will benefit you in all areas of life.

7

RANGE TIME AND DRILLS

RANGE TIME AND DRILLS ARE THE BREAD AND butter of a shooter's training regimen. They provide real-world applications for your skills and are essential for building confidence and improving accuracy. This chapter will dive deep into what you can expect during range sessions, offer comprehensive drills to enhance your technique and focus, and explain the importance of dry-firing and live-fire exercises. By the end of this chapter, you'll have a solid grasp of how to maximize your range sessions and drills to sharpen your shooting prowess.

INTRODUCTION TO RANGE TIME: WHAT TO EXPECT

Range time is a critical component of shooting practice, simulating real-life scenarios in a controlled environment. It allows you to apply techniques in real-time and assess your readiness for actual shooting situations. Knowing what to expect from range time helps you approach it with the right mindset, ensuring you make the most of each session.

Nancy Shooting Society - Common Room

PURPOSE OF RANGE TIME

- **Real-Time Application:** Range sessions let you practice shooting techniques and strategies against real targets. They help you understand how to apply skills learned during training and adjust based on the scenario at hand.
- **Real-World Experience:** The range gives you a taste of what it's like to shoot in various conditions, helping you manage things like recoil, trigger discipline, and sight alignment. This experience is invaluable for developing situational awareness and adaptability.
- **Confidence Building:** Regular range time builds confidence in your abilities. Testing your skills on the range helps you become more comfortable and assured with your firearm.

WHAT TO EXPECT

- **Controlled Environment:** Range sessions are typically conducted under the supervision of a range officer or instructor who sets the parameters for the session. The intensity can vary, from slow, deliberate shooting focused on technique to more dynamic drills simulating real-life conditions.
- **Communication with Range Officer:** Before starting, discuss the goals and rules with the range officer or instructor. Establish clear guidelines for the intensity of the session, such as focusing on accuracy, speed, or specific drills.
- **Focus on Technique:** Emphasize proper shooting techniques during range time rather than just hitting the target. Use each session as a learning experience to refine your skills and adapt to different shooting scenarios.
- **Safety and Respect:** Approach range time with respect for safety protocols and fellow shooters. Understand that it's a shared learning experience, and avoid any actions that could endanger yourself or others. Maintain good sportsmanship and use the opportunity to improve both your own skills and those of your peers.

PREPARING FOR RANGE TIME

- **Warm-Up:** A thorough warm-up is crucial before hitting the range. This can include some light stretching, dry-firing, and mental preparation to ensure you're ready for the physical and mental demands of the session.

- **Gear Check:** Ensure you have all the necessary gear,

including eye and ear protection, a proper firearm, ammunition, and any other safety equipment. Check that your firearm is in good working condition and properly maintained to prevent any mishaps.

DRILLS TO BUILD TECHNIQUE AND CONFIDENCE

Drills are essential for honing specific shooting skills and building confidence. They provide structured practice and allow you to focus on different aspects of your shooting technique. Here, we will explore various drills designed to improve your shooting abilities and prepare you for real-world scenarios.

Shooting with a Mauser 1909

Dry-Fire Drills

- **Purpose:** Dry-fire drills help you practice your trigger control, sight alignment, and grip without the need for live ammunition. They allow you to focus on form, consistency, and mental preparation.

- **Technique:**
  - *Trigger Control:* Practice smooth trigger pulls without disturbing the sights. Focus on steady, controlled movements.
  - *Sight Picture:* Maintain a proper sight picture throughout the trigger pull. This helps in developing muscle memory for accurate shooting.
- **Drills:**
  - *Wall Drill:* Stand close to a wall, aim at a small target, and practice dry-firing without moving the sights. This helps improve trigger discipline.
  - *Reset Drills:* Focus on resetting the trigger quickly and consistently after each dry-fire, preparing you for rapid follow-up shots.

Live-Fire Drills

- **Purpose:** Live-fire drills are where you apply all your training in a real-world environment. They develop power, accuracy, and endurance by simulating actual shooting conditions.
- **Technique:**
  - *Controlled Pairs:* Practice firing two shots in quick succession while maintaining accuracy. This drill helps build confidence in your ability to engage multiple targets quickly.
  - *Transition Drills:* Work on transitioning between targets smoothly and quickly. This helps improve your ability to engage multiple threats in rapid succession.

- **Drills:**
  - *Double Tap:* Focus on firing two shots in quick succession, ensuring both rounds hit the target. This drill builds muscle memory and confidence in your ability to shoot rapidly.
  - *Failure to Stop Drill:* Practice firing two shots to the chest and one to the head of the target. This drill is designed for high-stress scenarios where precision is critical.

Moving Target Drills

- **Purpose:** Moving target drills improve your ability to hit targets that are not stationary, simulating real-life shooting scenarios where your target might be on the move.
- **Technique:**
  - *Timing and Accuracy:* Work on hitting a moving target with precise timing. Focus on leading the target and adjusting for speed and distance.
  - *Combination Practice:* Practice different shooting positions and scenarios while engaging moving targets. This helps develop versatility and adaptability.
- **Drills:**
  - *Walking Target:* Engage a target that moves laterally across the range. Focus on timing and accuracy, leading the target properly to ensure a hit.
  - *Running Target:* Practice shooting at a target that moves quickly across your line of sight. This drill tests your reflexes and shooting accuracy under pressure.

PARTNER DRILLS FOR TIMING AND REACTION

Partner drills are essential for developing timing, reaction, and the ability to respond to dynamic scenarios. These drills help you practice techniques in a more unpredictable environment, enhancing your performance under pressure.

React and Engage

- **Purpose:** React and engage drills help improve your ability to quickly identify and engage targets under stress.
- **Technique:**
  - *Quick Reaction:* Respond quickly to your partner's signal to engage targets. This helps build the reflexes needed for high-pressure situations.
  - *Accuracy Under Pressure:* Focus on maintaining accuracy even when reacting quickly to unexpected scenarios.
- **Drills:**
  - *Pop-Up Targets:* Have your partner control pop-up targets, requiring you to engage them quickly and accurately. This simulates real-life scenarios where threats can appear suddenly.
  - *Reactive Drills:* Practice engaging targets that appear at random intervals, forcing you to react quickly and shoot accurately.

Range time and drills are crucial for developing and refining your shooting skills. Understanding what to expect from range sessions and incorporating a variety of drills into your training routine will significantly enhance your technique, confidence, and overall shooting performance.

RANGE TIME AND DRILLS

10 meters at the Olympic Games in 2016

By regularly practicing dry-firing, live-fire drills, moving target drills, and partner drills, you will build the skills needed for effective shooting in real-world conditions. Consistent practice and application of these techniques will lead to a more well-rounded and proficient shooter, ready to face any challenge.

SECTION THREE

CONDITIONING AND TRAINING

8

MENTAL CONDITIONING AND FOCUS ON SHOOTING SPORTS

SHOOTING SPORTS ARE NOT ONLY ABOUT PRECISION and physical skill but also about mental acuity and psychological resilience. Whether it's hitting a target at a long distance, managing pressure in a competition, or staying calm and collected during practice, the mental aspect of shooting is as crucial as the physical. This chapter delves into the importance of mental conditioning for shooters, exploring strategies for building concentration, resilience, visualization techniques, and methods for managing anxiety and maintaining focus. Developing a strong mental game is essential for peak performance and consistency in shooting sports.

THE MENTAL GAME IN SHOOTING SPORTS

Shooting sports demand a high level of mental discipline and concentration. The ability to maintain focus, manage stress, and stay composed under pressure can distinguish an average shooter from an exceptional one. Mental conditioning equips shooters with the tools to perform consistently and adapt to the dynamic nature of competitive shooting.

1. Importance of Mental Conditioning

- **Focus and Concentration:** In shooting, maintaining focus on the target and being able to execute a shot without distraction is crucial. Mental conditioning enhances concentration, enabling shooters to perform precise and deliberate actions.
- **Stress Management:** The competitive nature of shooting can be highly stressful. Whether it's the pressure of competition, environmental distractions, or the challenge of a new skill, managing stress effectively is key. Mental conditioning helps shooters remain calm, preventing stress from impairing performance.
- **Confidence:** Confidence in one's abilities, preparation, and equipment is vital in shooting sports. A confident shooter is more likely to make accurate shots and handle setbacks with composure. Mental conditioning strategies build and sustain this confidence, allowing for consistent performance.

In addition to these, mental conditioning also involves developing an understanding of how one's mind and body respond to different stimuli. For example, recognizing the signs of stress or anxiety early on can help a shooter implement techniques to mitigate these effects before they escalate, ensuring they remain in control throughout their performance.

2. Components of Mental Conditioning

- **Mental Toughness:** This is the ability to stay focused, resilient, and composed in challenging situations. Mental toughness allows shooters to handle pressure, recover from poor shots, and maintain a positive outlook even when things don't go as planned.
- **Emotional Regulation:** Managing emotions such as frustration, anxiety, or excitement is essential in shooting. Techniques for emotional regulation help shooters stay calm, avoid overreacting to mistakes, and maintain focus on the task at hand.
- **Goal Setting:** Setting realistic and achievable goals provides shooters with direction and motivation. Clear goals help maintain focus, track progress, and foster a sense of accomplishment.

Mental conditioning is also about building a routine that incorporates mental exercises, such as mindfulness and meditation, which can help shooters maintain a calm and focused mindset. By regularly practicing these techniques, shooters can train their minds to remain steady and composed, even in high-pressure situations.

BUILDING CONFIDENCE AND RESILIENCE IN SHOOTING SPORTS

Confidence and resilience are critical attributes for success in shooting sports. Confidence stems from a strong belief in one's skills and preparation, while resilience enables shooters to bounce back from mistakes and setbacks.

1. Developing Confidence

- **Preparation and Practice:** Confidence is built through consistent and deliberate practice. Knowing that you have prepared thoroughly for a competition or practice session allows you to trust your skills and approach each shot with assurance.
- **Positive Self-Talk:** Replacing negative thoughts with positive affirmations can significantly impact performance. Remind yourself of your strengths, previous successes, and the effort you've invested in training.
- **Visualizing Success:** Visualization techniques reinforce confidence by allowing shooters to mentally rehearse successful outcomes. By imagining yourself hitting targets accurately and smoothly, you can boost your belief in your ability to perform under pressure.

Developing confidence also involves confronting and overcoming one's fears. Shooters may have to deal with the fear of failure, the fear of letting down their team, or even the fear of injury. By facing these fears head-on, rather than avoiding them, shooters can build a stronger sense of self-assurance and resilience Developing confidence also involves confronting and overcoming one's fears. Shooters may have to deal with the fear of failure, the fear of letting down their team, or even the fear of injury. By facing these fears head-on, rather than avoiding them, shooters can build a stronger sense of self-assurance and resilience

2. Building Resilience

- **Embracing Challenges:** View challenges and setbacks as opportunities for growth rather than obstacles. Overcoming difficulties in training and competition builds resilience, making you better equipped to handle future challenges.
- **Learning from Mistakes:** Treat mistakes and missed shots as learning experiences. Analyze what went wrong, make the necessary adjustments, and apply these lessons to improve your technique and mental approach.
- **Maintaining Perspective:** Keep a balanced view of successes and failures. Understand that both are integral to your development as a shooter and that each experience contributes to your overall growth.

Resilience is also about maintaining motivation and perseverance, even when progress is slow or setbacks occur. By keeping the long-term goal in mind and focusing on incremental improvements, shooters can stay motivated and resilient in the face of adversity.

VISUALIZATION TECHNIQUES FOR SUCCESS IN SHOOTING

Visualization is a powerful tool used by athletes to enhance performance. By vividly imagining successful outcomes and scenarios, shooters can improve their focus, confidence, and overall performance.

1. Understanding Visualization

- **Definition:** Visualization involves creating a detailed mental image of yourself performing successfully. For shooters, this means imagining hitting targets perfectly, maintaining steady aim, and executing shots flawlessly.
- **Mechanism:** Repeated visualization of successful shooting scenarios trains the mind to react positively and confidently in real-life situations, reinforcing neural pathways associated with performance.

Visualization also helps in reducing anxiety by preparing the mind for the pressure of competition. By mentally rehearsing each step of the competition, shooters can approach the actual event with a sense of familiarity and confidence.

2. Techniques for Effective Visualization

- **Detailed Imagery:** Close your eyes and imagine every aspect of your shooting environment—the feel of the gun, the sight picture, the sound of the range, and the process of taking a perfect shot. Visualize your breathing, stance, and trigger pull, and see the bullet hitting the center of the target.
- **Positive Scenarios:** Focus on positive outcomes, such as achieving high scores, winning a competition, or mastering a difficult technique. Visualization should always reinforce success, helping to build confidence and reduce performance anxiety.
- **Repetition:** Practice visualization regularly in a quiet and relaxed environment. Consistency is key to making visualization a part of your mental conditioning routine.

Over time, this mental rehearsal will make your actions more automatic and confident in real-life scenarios.

Visualization can also be used to mentally rehearse different strategies and scenarios, helping shooters prepare for various potential challenges they may face during competition

3. Applying Visualization

- **Before Practice:** Use visualization to mentally prepare for practice sessions. Imagine yourself executing drills and exercises with precision and ease, which helps set a positive tone for your practice.
- **Before Competitions:** Visualize the entire competition process, from preparing your equipment to stepping onto the shooting line, executing your shots, and achieving your goals. This comprehensive mental rehearsal helps reduce anxiety and prepares you for every aspect of the event.
- **During Practice:** Incorporate visualization into your practice by mentally rehearsing specific techniques or scenarios. For instance, visualize a perfect shot sequence before physically performing it, enhancing your mental focus and confidence.

MANAGING ANXIETY AND MAINTAINING FOCUS IN SHOOTING SPORTS

Anxiety and nerves are natural reactions to competition and high-pressure situations. Learning to manage these emotions is essential for maintaining focus and achieving optimal performance in shooting sports.

MENTAL CONDITIONING AND FOCUS ON SHOOTING

1. Understanding Anxiety in Shooting

- **Sources:** Anxiety in shooting can arise from various sources, such as the fear of missing a target, the pressure of competition, or the desire to meet personal or external expectations.
- **Effects:** Anxiety can negatively impact focus, motor control, and decision-making, leading to missed shots and inconsistent performance. Effective management of anxiety is crucial to maintaining control and achieving peak performance.

Understanding anxiety also involves recognizing the physical symptoms, such as increased heart rate, sweating, or shaking, and learning how to control these physiological responses through techniques such as deep-breathing or progressive muscle relaxation

2. Strategies for Managing Anxiety

- **Breathing Techniques:** Practice deep breathing exercises to calm the nervous system and reduce anxiety. Focusing on slow, controlled breaths can help relax the body and clear the mind, enhancing concentration.
  - *Example Exercise:* Inhale deeply through your nose for a count of four, hold the breath for four counts, and exhale slowly through your mouth for a count of six. Repeat this process several times to calm your mind and body.
- **Mindfulness and Relaxation:** Engage in mindfulness practices to stay present and focused on the moment.

Techniques such as meditation, progressive muscle relaxation, or simply focusing on the sensations of your breath can help manage anxiety and improve concentration.

- *Mindfulness Practice:* Spend a few minutes each day sitting quietly, focusing on your breathing or the feeling of your body in space. This practice builds awareness and control over your thoughts and emotions, making it easier to stay calm and focused during competition.

- **Pre-Competition Routine:** Develop a pre-competition routine that includes relaxation techniques and mental preparation. A consistent routine creates a sense of control and familiarity, helping to reduce anxiety before stepping onto the range.
  - *Routine Elements:* Your routine might include listening to calming music, performing gentle stretching exercises, reviewing your shooting plan, or engaging in positive self-talk.

- **Positive Visualization:** Use visualization to combat anxiety by imagining calm, controlled, and successful performance scenarios. By focusing on positive outcomes, you can shift attention away from fear and reinforce confidence.
  - *Visualizing Calmness:* Imagine yourself remaining calm and composed, even in high-pressure situations. Visualize handling challenges with poise and executing each shot confidently.

3. Seeking Support

- **Mental Coaching:** Consider working with a sports psychologist or mental coach who specializes in shooting sports. They can help develop personalized strategies for managing anxiety, building confidence, and improving mental toughness.
- **Support Network:** Surround yourself with supportive individuals who understand the challenges of shooting sports. Share your experiences, seek advice, and draw encouragement from coaches, teammates, and mentors who can provide perspective and motivation.

In the intricate world of shooting sports, where precision meets passion, mental conditioning emerges as an unsung hero. It is the thread that weaves together the physical prowess and psychological resilience necessary to hit the mark, both literally and figuratively. As we approach the end of our investigation into the mental aspect of shooting, it becomes evident that this aspect of training not only supplements physical practice, but serves as the fundamental foundation for achieving exceptional performance.

Mental conditioning in shooting is like calibrating a finely tuned instrument. Just as a shooter meticulously adjusts their sights to ensure accuracy, so too must they fine-tune their mind to maintain focus and composure under pressure. It is this mental precision that distinguishes the good from the great, transforming competent shooters into champions. The mental arena is where the true battle is fought, where the internal dialogs, visualizations, and stress management techniques culminate in a single, perfect shot.

At the heart of mental conditioning lies the art of concentration. In the world of shooting, where every millisecond counts and every movement is scrutinized, the ability to sustain focus is paramount. Concentration is not a passive state but an active engagement of the mind, a deliberate narrowing of awareness to the essentials: breath, target, and timing. This heightened focus is cultivated through persistent mental exercises, mindfulness practices, and a relentless commitment to blocking out distractions. Over time, this practice sharpens the mind to a fine point, allowing shooters to enter a state of flow where the world falls away, leaving only the target in their sight.

But concentration alone is not enough. Resilience—the mental armor that shields against the inevitable pressures of the sport—is equally crucial. The shooting range is a crucible of stress, where the weight of competition and the sting of missed shots can easily erode confidence. Resilience is the buffer that absorbs these shocks, enabling shooters to recover quickly and maintain their composure. It is the inner strength that turns setbacks into comebacks, the quiet resolve that keeps the shooter's hand steady even when their heart is racing. Through mental toughness exercises and exposure to challenging scenarios, shooters build a reservoir of resilience that they can draw upon in the heat of competition.

Visualization, too, plays a pivotal role in the shooter's mental arsenal. This technique, often likened to mental rehearsal, allows shooters to pre-experience success in their mind's eye. By vividly imagining each step of their routine—the feel of the gun, the alignment of the sights, the smooth pull of the trigger—shooters reinforce the neural pathways that govern their performance. Visualization is more than just daydreaming; it is a form of mental training that makes success feel familiar and attainable. It cultivates confidence by enabling shooters to repeatedly envision themselves succeeding, enabling them to perform with calm assurance when the crucial moment arrives.

Anxiety management, the final cornerstone of mental conditioning, is perhaps the most challenging to master. The background shadow of anxiety is ready to attack at the first sign of weakness. In a sport where even the slightest tremor can mean the difference between victory and defeat, managing anxiety is not just beneficial—it's essential. Techniques such as deep breathing, progressive muscle relaxation, and mindfulness meditation serve as the antidotes to this ever-present threat. These practices calm the body's physiological responses to stress, allowing the mind to remain clear and focused. Positive self-talk and affirmations further assist in redirecting the mind away from fear and towards a state of readiness and confidence.

As we reflect on the mental conditioning required for shooting sports, it becomes evident that this aspect of training is about more than just improving performance. It is about cultivating a mindset that allows shooters to truly enjoy the sport, to approach each shot with a sense of calm and control, and to remain adaptable in the face of ever-changing conditions. This mental fortitude extends beyond the shooting range, equipping individuals with the tools to navigate life's challenges with the same focus, resilience, and composure that they bring to their sport.

In conclusion, the journey to becoming an elite shooter is as much a mental one as it is physical. Mental conditioning is not an optional extra; it is an integral part of the training process that must be prioritized if one is to achieve excellence in shooting sports. By focusing on the mental game—developing concentration, resilience, visualization, and anxiety management—shooters can unlock their full potential. This holistic approach to training ensures that they are not only physically prepared but also mentally and emotionally equipped to face the challenges of the sport. In doing so, they can achieve their goals and enjoy a long and successful shooting career where each shot shows the mind's power and the hand's skill.

Meerut shooting team, 106th Hazara Pioneers, 1912 (c)

9

PHYSICAL CONDITIONING FOR SHOOTERS

PHYSICAL CONDITIONING IS CRUCIAL IN SHOOTING sports, enhancing stability, accuracy, endurance, and overall performance. Unlike other sports that focus on power or speed, conditioning for shooters requires a comprehensive approach that integrates cardiovascular fitness, strength training, flexibility, mobility, and effective recovery. These elements work together to optimize fine motor skills, precision, and mental acuity, enabling shooters to perform at their best. This chapter explores these conditioning aspects, offering strategies to build a foundation for sustained success in the sport.

THE IMPORTANCE OF CARDIOVASCULAR FITNESS FOR SHOOTERS

Cardiovascular fitness is vital for shooters as it affects stamina, focus, and the ability to maintain control under physical and mental stress. A strong cardiovascular system supports sustained focus during long matches and aids in maintaining a steady heart rate, which is critical for accuracy.

Nancy Johnson (red visor) competes in women's 10m air rifle at the 2000 Sydney Olympics

1. Benefits of Cardiovascular Fitness:

- **Endurance:** Cardiovascular fitness enhances your ability to maintain energy levels during extended shooting sessions or competitions. This endurance is critical for staying sharp, making accurate shots, and managing the physical demands of moving through different shooting positions.
- **Stress Management:** A well-conditioned cardiovascular system helps regulate stress and anxiety levels, which can impact heart rate and stability. Controlling your heart rate is essential for precision, especially in high-stakes scenarios.

- **Recovery:** Improved cardiovascular health aids in quicker recovery from physical exertion, whether moving between shooting stages or managing the physical load of equipment.

2. Cardiovascular Training Methods:

- **Steady-State Cardio:** Activities such as walking, cycling, and rowing at a moderate pace improve overall cardiovascular health. Aim for 20 to 30 minutes of steady-state cardio, 3 to 4 times per week, to build a strong aerobic base.

One-third paper target for fullbore competitions in Nordic Field Shooting

- **Interval Training:** High-Intensity Interval Training (HIIT) involves short bursts of intense exercise

followed by periods of lower intensity or rest. This method improves cardiovascular capacity and simulates the bursts of activity common in practical shooting scenarios. For example, sprint for 30 seconds followed by a 1-minute walk, and repeat for 20 minutes.
- **Sport-Specific Drills:** Incorporate drills like shuttle runs or obstacle courses to mimic the movement patterns and intensity of shooting competitions. These activities enhance cardiovascular fitness while directly improving skills relevant to shooting sports.

3. Incorporating Cardio into Your Training:

- **Warm-Up:** Use light cardiovascular exercises as part of your warm-up routine to prepare your body for shooting practice. This helps elevate your heart rate gradually, improving blood flow to muscles and enhancing overall performance.
- **Consistency:** Regularly incorporate cardio sessions into your weekly training plan to maintain and build endurance. Adjust the intensity and duration based on your specific goals and the demands of your shooting discipline.

STRENGTH TRAINING FOR SHOOTERS

Strength training is essential for improving the physical control and stability needed in shooting sports. A well-rounded strength program focuses on enhancing the muscles used in holding and maneuvering firearms, as well as maintaining posture during shooting.

1. Benefits of Strength Training:

- **Stability and Control:** Strength training improves your ability to maintain steady positions, whether standing, kneeling, or prone. Strong core and back muscles are particularly important for stability, allowing you to manage recoil effectively and keep your aim steady.
- **Recoil Management:** Increased upper body strength helps manage recoil, reducing muzzle rise and allowing quicker follow-up shots. A strong grip and forearm strength are particularly beneficial for managing the force of repeated firing.
- **Reduced Fatigue:** Strengthening the muscles used in holding and aiming firearms helps reduce fatigue during extended shooting sessions, leading to better accuracy over time.

2. Key Strength Training Exercises:

- **Upper Body:**
    - *Shoulder Presses:* Use dumbbells or a barbell to perform overhead presses, strengthening the shoulders and upper back muscles crucial for holding and aiming firearms.
    - *Rows:* Bent-over rows or seated rows target the back muscles, enhancing your ability to stabilize and control your firearm during shooting.
    - *Grip Strengthening:* Exercises like wrist curls, farmer's walks, and squeezing grip trainers build forearm strength, essential for maintaining a firm grip on your firearm.

- **Lower Body:**
  - *Squats:* Bodyweight or weighted squats build leg strength, supporting stable stances and transitions between shooting positions.
  - *Step-Ups:* Step-ups improve leg strength and balance, aiding in movement and positioning during dynamic shooting stages.
- **Core:**
  - *Planks:* Planks and side planks strengthen the core muscles, providing the stability needed for accurate shooting from various positions.
  - *Russian Twists:* This exercise targets the obliques, enhancing rotational strength and stability during dynamic shooting movements.

3. Structuring Your Strength Training:

- **Frequency:** Incorporate strength training sessions 2 to 3 times per week, allowing adequate rest between workouts. Balance strength training with shooting practice to ensure comprehensive development without overtraining.
- **Progression:** Gradually increase weights and intensity to continue making progress. Focus on maintaining proper form to maximize benefits and minimize the risk of injury.
- **Integration:** Combine strength training with other conditioning elements, such as cardiovascular and flexibility workouts, to create a balanced and effective training program.

FLEXIBILITY AND MOBILITY WORKOUTS FOR SHOOTERS

Flexibility and mobility are essential for shooters, aiding in full range of motion, injury prevention, and improved performance. Agility and flexibility are key to executing techniques effectively and adapting to various shooting positions.

- **Importance:**
    - *Range of Motion:* Enhanced flexibility allows optimal shooting positions, improving aim and posture.
    - *Injury Prevention:* Flexible muscles and joints reduce the risk of strains and injuries, maintaining peak condition.
    - *Performance Enhancement:* Flexibility and mobility improve efficiency and stability, crucial for quick transitions and effective aiming.
- **Flexibility Exercises:**
    - *Static Stretching:* Perform after workouts, focusing on shoulders, back, legs, and arms.
        - *Shoulder Stretch:* Pull one arm across the chest.
        - *Hamstring Stretch:* Reach for toes with one leg extended.
        - *Quadriceps Stretch:* Pull ankle towards glutes.
    - *Dynamic Stretching:* Use during warm-up with leg swings, arm circles, and torso twists.
- **Mobility Workouts:**
    - *Foam Rolling:* Reduce muscle tightness and enhance mobility.
    - *Joint Mobility Drills:* Include hip circles, shoulder rotations, and ankle rolls.

- *Yoga:* Incorporate poses like downward dog and warrior for flexibility and relaxation.
- **Routine Structure:**
  - *Frequency:* Perform 3-4 times per week, integrating into warm-up and cool-down sessions.
  - *Consistency:* Gradually increase duration and intensity for ongoing improvement.

REST AND RECOVERY: ESSENTIAL FOR PEAK PERFORMANCE

Rest and recovery are critical components of any training program, allowing your body to repair and strengthen, reducing the risk of overtraining and injury.

1. Importance of Rest and Recovery:

- **Muscle Repair:** Rest is essential for muscle recovery and growth. Adequate rest periods allow your body to repair after intense training sessions, improving overall strength and endurance.
- **Injury Prevention:** Proper recovery helps prevent overuse injuries and reduces the risk of burnout, supporting long-term participation and success in shooting sports.
- **Performance Optimization:** Sufficient rest improves focus, energy levels, and physical readiness, ensuring you are at your best for training sessions and competitions.

2. Strategies for Effective Recovery:

- **Rest Days:** Incorporate at least one full rest day per week into your training schedule. Use this time to recover

fully and engage in light activities such as walking or stretching to maintain mobility.
- **Sleep:** Prioritize quality sleep to support recovery. Aim for 7 to 9 hours of sleep per night, establishing a regular sleep schedule to enhance muscle repair and overall well-being.
- **Nutrition:** A balanced diet rich in protein, carbohydrates, and healthy fats supports muscle repair and replenishes energy stores. Consider post-workout meals with adequate protein and carbs to boost recovery.
- **Hydration:** Maintain proper hydration before, during, and after training. Water supports muscle function and recovery, and staying hydrated is essential for peak physical performance.

3. Monitoring and Avoiding Overtraining:

- **Recognize: Symptoms:** Be aware of overtraining symptoms such as persistent fatigue, reduced performance, and increased susceptibility to injuries. Adjust your training intensity and schedule as needed to prevent overtraining.
- **Listen to Your Body:** Pay attention to how your body feels during and after workouts. Modify your training based on your physical condition and recovery needs to avoid burnout and maximize performance.
- **Consult Professionals:** Work with a coach or trainer to develop a balanced training plan that includes proper rest and recovery strategies. Their guidance can help tailor your program to your specific needs and goals.

10

NUTRITION AND DIET FOR SHOOTING SPORTS

NUTRITION PLAYS A PIVOTAL ROLE IN SHOOTING sports, much like it does in any other physical discipline. It's not just about eating the right foods; it's a precise blend of science and strategy that fuels a shooter's performance, sharpens focus, enhances endurance, and aids in quick recovery. For shooters, every meal and snack is an opportunity to improve concentration, stabilize energy levels, and support the body's ability to perform

Sport-shooting with air-rifles 10m

consistently under pressure. This chapter delves into the nuances of nutrition tailored specifically for shooting sports, covering essential nutrients, how to structure a balanced diet, hydration strategies, and how to adjust your nutrition plan for training and competition days.

THE ROLE OF NUTRITION IN SHOOTING SPORTS PERFORMANCE

Nutrition is the foundation for peak performance in shooting sports. Proper dietary habits ensure that the body and mind are primed for the demands of training and competition, providing sustained energy, improving focus, and supporting overall health and resilience.

Enhancing Focus and Mental Clarity

Importance: In shooting sports, mental clarity and sharp focus are paramount. Proper nutrition supports cognitive function, helping shooters maintain concentration, make precise decisions, and manage stress during competitions.

Key Nutrients:

- **Omega-3 Fatty Acids:** Found in fish like salmon and mackerel, as well as flaxseeds and walnuts, omega-3s enhance brain function, improve mood, and reduce anxiety—critical factors for shooters who must maintain calm under pressure.
- **Antioxidants:** Foods rich in antioxidants, such as berries, dark chocolate, and green leafy vegetables, help reduce oxidative stress and improve brain health, supporting sustained mental performance and faster

cognitive recovery from high-pressure situations.
- **B Vitamins:** These vitamins, particularly B6, B12, and folate, are crucial for brain function, energy production, and mood regulation. Whole grains, eggs, and leafy greens are excellent sources to ensure adequate intake, supporting neurotransmitter function and overall mental sharpness.

SUSTAINING ENERGY AND STAMINA

Importance: Maintaining stable energy levels throughout long training sessions or competitions is essential for consistent performance. Energy dips can lead to fatigue, reduced concentration, and diminished performance.

Shooting at the 2018 Summer Youth Olympics – 10m Air Rifle Mixed International Victory Ceremony

Key Nutrients:

- **Complex Carbohydrates:** Foods such as whole grains, oats, sweet potatoes, and quinoa provide a steady release of glucose, helping sustain energy levels without the spikes and crashes associated with simple sugars. This is particularly important for shooters, who need to maintain steady hands and focused attention over long periods.
- **Proteins:** Adequate protein intake is essential for muscle repair and growth, even in shooting sports, where muscle endurance and stability play roles. Lean meats, fish, eggs, and plant-based proteins like beans and tofu help maintain muscle mass, which supports stable shooting posture and stamina.
- **Healthy Fats:** Incorporate healthy fats like those found in avocados, nuts, seeds, and olive oil, which provide long-lasting energy and assist in the absorption of fat-soluble vitamins that are essential for overall health. These fats are also important for maintaining a healthy nervous system, which supports fine motor skills crucial for shooting.

Micronutrients: Supporting Performance and Recovery

- **Vitamins and Minerals:** Essential for energy production, immune function, and recovery. Specific nutrients like iron, calcium, vitamin D, and magnesium play pivotal roles:
    - *Iron:* Important for oxygen transport in the blood, which is crucial for sustained energy and endurance.

Include iron-rich foods like lean meats, beans, spinach, and fortified cereals to support your body's endurance needs.

- *Calcium and Vitamin D:* These support bone health and muscle function, vital for stability and posture in shooting. Sources include dairy products, leafy greens, and fortified foods.
- *Magnesium:* Involved in muscle relaxation and preventing cramps, magnesium can be found in nuts, seeds, whole grains, and dark chocolate. It also supports a calm nervous system, aiding in the precision and steady hand required in shooting.

HYDRATION STRATEGIES FOR SHOOTERS

Proper hydration is critical in shooting sports as it directly affects concentration, reaction time, and overall physical comfort. Dehydration can impair cognitive function and physical performance, making it crucial to develop effective hydration strategies.

Daily Hydration Needs

- **Baseline Intake:** Aim for 2.5 to 3 liters of fluids per day, including water, herbal teas, and hydrating foods like fruits and vegetables. Adjust based on climate, activity level, and individual needs.
- **Signs of Dehydration:** Common symptoms include headache, fatigue, dizziness, and difficulty concentrating. Monitor urine color as a simple hydration check; pale yellow is optimal.

ADJUSTING NUTRITION FOR WEIGHT MANAGEMENT

For shooters who compete in weight-classed events, managing weight while maintaining performance can be challenging. A strategic approach to nutrition can help achieve the desired weight safely without compromising energy or focus.

Safe Weight Management Strategies

- **Gradual Changes:** Aim for gradual weight adjustments rather than drastic cuts. A weekly reduction of 0.5-1 kg is generally safe and sustainable.
- **Balanced Diet:** Focus on nutrient-dense, low-calorie foods that provide essential nutrients without excess calories. This includes lean proteins, plenty of vegetables, whole grains, and healthy fats.
- **Hydration Management:** Be cautious with rapid weight loss methods involving dehydration, as they can impair cognitive function and performance. Rehydrate appropriately after weighing in to restore fluid balance.

Professional Guidance

- **Consultation:** Work with a nutritionist or dietitian specializing in sports to develop a personalized nutrition and weight management plan. Regular assessments and adjustments ensure the plan remains effective and safe.
- **Monitoring Progress:** Track dietary intake, weight changes, performance metrics, and overall well-being to ensure that weight management strategies do not negatively impact performance or health.

SECTION FOUR

ADVANCED TECHNIQUES AND STRATEGY

11

PRECISION MASTERY: ADVANCED SHOOTING SKILLS

MASTERING ADVANCED SHOOTING TECHNIQUES IS essential for developing a sophisticated and effective shooting style in competitive sports. As you progress from basic skills to more complex techniques, you'll enhance your ability to control the pace, adapt to varying conditions, exploit your opponent's weaknesses, and execute precision shots with confidence. This chapter provides an in-depth exploration of advanced shooting techniques, including shooting in challenging conditions, utilizing specialized shooting positions, breathing control, timing, and the strategic use of mental visualization to enhance performance.

SHOOTING IN CHALLENGING CONDITIONS

Competitive shooting often involves dealing with a variety of environmental factors that can impact performance. Wind, light conditions, and even the pressure of the competition

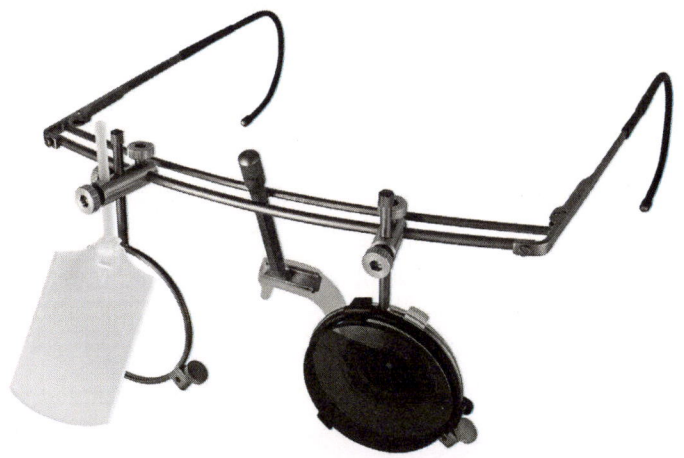

Shooting glasses used as a visual aid for sport shooting

can pose significant challenges. Learning to adapt to these conditions are crucial for maintaining accuracy and consistency.

1. Shooting in Windy Conditions

- **Understanding Wind Patterns:** Wind can significantly alter the trajectory of a bullet. Understanding how wind speed and direction affect your shots is the first step in mastering this advanced skill.
  - *Wind Reading:* Learn to read the wind using visual cues like the movement of trees, flags, or mirage patterns on the range. Identifying the strength and direction of the wind allows you to make necessary adjustments.
  - *Adjusting for Wind:* Adjustments can be made by holding off the target or dialing windage corrections

into your sight. Practice compensating for wind by shooting in varied wind conditions, adjusting your aim based on your wind reading.

2. Managing Light Conditions

- **Shooting in Low Light:** Low light conditions can affect visibility and your ability to see the target clearly. Use of specialized equipment such as illuminated reticles or night vision can help, but understanding and adapting to the light conditions is key.
  - *Equipment:* Utilize sights and scopes designed for low light, such as those with illuminated reticles. Ensure that your equipment is correctly zeroed for the specific light conditions.
  - *Techniques:* Learn to adjust your shooting posture and breathing to reduce glare and enhance visibility. Practice in varied light conditions to build familiarity and confidence.
- **Dealing with Glare:** Glare from the sun or artificial lights can be distracting and impair your sight picture. Utilize visors, sunshades on scopes, or position yourself to minimize the impact of glare on your shooting.
  - *Position Adjustments:* Adjust your shooting stance or position to shield your eyes from direct glare. Understanding how to use available shadows or positioning can significantly improve your visual clarity.

3. Managing Stress and Pressure

- **Simulating Competition Pressure:** Stress and pressure can affect your shooting performance. Simulate

competition scenarios during practice to build resilience. Incorporate time limits, audience noise, or other stressors to replicate the conditions of a real competition.
  - *Mental Rehearsal:* Use visualization to mentally rehearse competition scenarios. Practice imagining yourself handling the pressure calmly, executing your shots with confidence, and recovering from any mistakes quickly.
- **Controlled Breathing:** Develop controlled breathing techniques to maintain calm and focus. Controlled breathing lowers heart rate and reduces the physical symptoms of stress, such as shaking or tension.
  - *Box Breathing Technique:* Inhale deeply for four counts, hold for four counts, exhale for four counts, and hold again for four counts. This method can help calm nerves and steady your hands before taking a shot.

UTILIZING SPECIALIZED SHOOTING POSITIONS

Mastering a range of shooting positions is crucial for adapting to different scenarios and maximizing accuracy. Advanced shooting positions go beyond the basics, allowing for greater flexibility and precision.

MASTERING BREATHING CONTROL

Breathing control is a fundamental skill in shooting that directly impacts accuracy. Proper breathing techniques help shooters maintain steadiness and reduce the body's natural movements that can affect aim.

SECTION FIVE

THE ART OF COMPETITIVE MARKSMANSHIP

12

PREPARING FOR YOUR FIRST SHOOTING COMPETITION

PREPARING FOR YOUR FIRST SHOOTING competition is more than just an event on your calendar; it's a milestone that reflects the culmination of your hard work, dedication, and relentless pursuit of excellence in shooting. It's a moment that bridges practice and performance, turning theory into action. In this chapter, we'll dive deeply into the comprehensive preparations required to excel in your debut, focusing on the intricate blend of technical skill, mental toughness, and logistical planning. By mastering these aspects, you will approach your first competition not just with readiness, but with a sense of poise and purpose.

THE PATH TO YOUR FIRST COMPETITIVE SHOOT

Your journey to the shooting range on competition day is a series of carefully orchestrated steps that together build the foundation for success. Each phase is crucial, from the

PREPARING FOR YOUR FIRST SHOOTING COMPETITION

basics of training to the advanced nuances of competition strategy. Let's explore this path in detail to ensure that no stone is left unturned in your preparation.

BUILDING A STRONG FOUNDATION

Structured Training Regimen

A well-rounded training regimen is the backbone of competitive shooting. It's not just about firing shots; it's about methodically honing every aspect of your performance. Begin by designing a comprehensive training plan that includes technical drills, equipment handling, physical conditioning, and mental preparation. Divide your weekly schedule to allocate time

Stamp of Indonesia–1984– Gun shooting

Shooting sports- Iran

for critical skills such as sight alignment, trigger control, and breath management. Each session should have a clear objective, whether it's improving reaction time, refining accuracy, or enhancing endurance. Consistency and repetition will build the muscle memory needed under competition pressure.

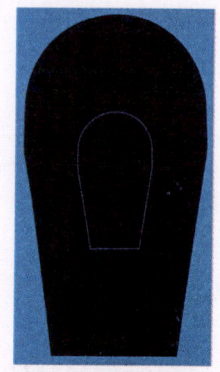

Paper target for fullbore competitions in Nordic Field Shooting

Technical Skills Mastery

Your technical proficiency in shooting directly influences your performance.

Physical Conditioning

Shooting sports demand more physical prowess than one might initially assume. Endurance, stability, and core strengths are essential for maintaining accuracy and focus throughout prolonged events. A comprehensive conditioning routine should include:

- **Cardiovascular Training:** Engage in regular cardio exercises such as running, cycling, or rowing. These activities improve overall stamina, enabling you to maintain composure and performance during lengthy competitions.
- **Strength Training:** Emphasize exercises that enhance core stability, upper body strength, and grip endurance. Weightlifting, resistance bands, and functional movements like planks and push-ups are particularly beneficial.
- **Flexibility and Mobility:** Flexibility contributes to better shooting posture and reduces the risk of injury.

Incorporate stretching routines, yoga, or dynamic warm-ups into your training to keep your muscles agile and ready for varied shooting positions.

FINDING AND REGISTERING FOR COMPETITIONS

Identifying Events

Choose events that align with your current skill set and provide a clear progression path to more advanced levels. If possible, attend as a spectator before competing to familiarize yourself with the atmosphere and format.

Understanding Eligibility

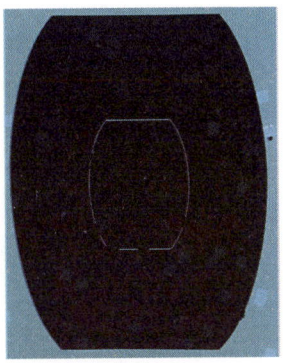

Barrel paper target for fullbore competitions in Nordic Field Shooting

Competitions often have specific eligibility criteria, including membership in shooting associations, completion of safety certifications, and adherence to age or equipment standards. Thoroughly review the requirements for each event to ensure compliance. Missteps here can lead to disqualification or missed opportunities, so confirm your status well in advance and rectify any deficiencies.

Registration Process

Timely registration is critical to secure your spot in the competition. Registration usually involves completing detailed forms, submitting entry fees, and providing proof of eligibility. Double-check all information before submission to avoid administrative issues. Once registered, make a point to study the event schedule, familiarize yourself with the venue layout, and note key logistics such as check-in times and locations. Having these details in hand will alleviate pre-event stress and help you focus on your performance.

PRE-COMPETITION PREPARATIONS

Training Tapering

As competition day nears, reduce workout volume while keeping key skills sharp. Avoid overtraining, which can lead to fatigue. Focus on light drills, visualization, and routine maintenance to stay rested yet ready.

Mental Preparation

Mental readiness is as crucial as physical. Regularly practice visualization, seeing yourself succeed and handling challenges. Incorporate relaxation techniques like deep breathing and meditation to build resilience against competition nerves.

Equipment Check and Logistics

Ensure all equipment is in top condition well before the event. Thoroughly inspect firearms, ammunition, and safety gear. Clean and test everything and pack an emergency kit with spare parts and tools to avoid any last-minute issues.

Consider the logistics of your journey—whether it's a short drive or requires travel arrangements, and ensure every aspect is planned to avoid last-minute complications.

WHAT TO EXPECT ON COMPETITION DAY

Understanding the flow of competition day is crucial for managing stress and maintaining focus. Knowing what to anticipate allows you to navigate the day with composure and confidence.

Shooting sports in Iran

ON THE FIRING LINE

Routine and Focus

Establishing a pre-shooting routine can be a powerful tool for maintaining consistency. Whether it's a sequence of physical actions, a mental mantra, or a deep breathing pattern, a routine helps center your focus and calm your nerves. Develop a routine that works for you and stick to it throughout the competition to create a sense of familiarity and control.

Managing Pressure

The pressure of competition is a given, and managing it effectively is key to success. Acknowledge the nerves as a natural response to the stakes involved. Instead of fighting them, channel that energy into heightened awareness and precision. Break down your task to the immediate goal—execute each shot with deliberate focus, ignoring the broader implications of score or ranking. Keep your mind in the present, shot by shot.

Spc. Daniel Lowe 34th in Rio Games air rifle

HANDLING COMPETITION NERVES

Recognizing Normalcy

It's important to recognize that nerves are a universal experience in competition. They signify your commitment and investment in your performance. Accepting nerves as a normal part of the process can diminish their power over you. Instead of perceiving them as a threat, view them as a sign that you care deeply about doing well.

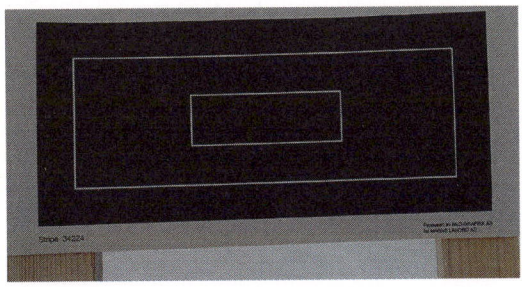

Stripe paper target for smallbore competitions in Nordic Field Shooting

Channeling Nervous Energy

Nervous energy can be redirected to enhance your performance. Use the adrenaline boost to sharpen your concentration and quicken your reflexes. Stay engaged with each shot, focusing on execution rather than outcome. This shift in mindset can turn what feels like a disadvantage into a performance-enhancing state.

Laser Pistols (UIPM homologated) for Modern Pentathlon, Laser Run and Triathle

Relaxation Techniques

Incorporate relaxation techniques into your pre-competition routine. Methods like deep breathing, progressive muscle relaxation, or mindfulness meditation can help keep anxiety at manageable levels. Regular practice of these techniques will make them second nature, ready to be deployed when competition stress peaks.

THE ROLE OF YOUR SUPPORT TEAM

Your support team—whether it's a coach, mentor, or encouraging friends and family—plays an integral role in your journey. Their contributions extend beyond mere presence; they provide strategic guidance, emotional backing, and practical assistance.

KOCIS London Korea Jinjongoh Shooting

Pre-Competition Support

In the lead-up to your competition, your support team can be invaluable. Coaches can offer expert advice on strategy

PREPARING FOR YOUR FIRST SHOOTING COMPETITION

and technique, while friends and family can provide the emotional encouragement that bolsters confidence. Use their insights to refine your approach, and lean on their experience to navigate pre-competition challenges.

On-Site Guidance

During the competition, your support team serves as a steadying presence. They can offer quick tips between stages, help troubleshoot any equipment issues, and provide moral support to keep you grounded. Their observations from the sidelines can offer fresh perspectives and immediate feedback, helping you stay adaptable in real-time.

Shooting team of Socialist Republic of Bosnia and Herzegovina at competition in Bucharest 1973

13

ANALYZING COMPETITIONS AND LEARNING FROM EXPERIENCE

ANALYSING COMPETITIONS AND LEARNING FROM experiences is crucial for any shooter aspiring to advance in their sport. Whether you are involved in rifle, pistol, or shotgun disciplines, understanding the intricacies of competitive performance through detailed analysis helps refine skills, improve strategies, and achieve consistency. This chapter provides an extensive guide on how to analyze professional competitions, review your own performances, utilize video effectively, and learn from both successes and setbacks. Mastering these aspects will significantly enhance your shooting capabilities and strategic approach.

OBSERVING AND LEARNING FROM PROFESSIONAL COMPETITIONS

Watching professional shooting competitions provides invaluable insights into advanced techniques, strategic planning, and in-competition behavior. Here's how to make the most of this learning opportunity:

1. Observing Techniques and Disciplines

- **Technical Precision:** Professional shooters display exceptional technical skills that are vital for success. Focus on how they maintain sight alignment, control their breathing, and execute trigger pulls with precision. Observe how they achieve consistency across various shots and stages, especially under pressure.
- **Diverse Shooting Disciplines:** Each shooting discipline has unique requirements, from precision rifle shooting to fast-paced action pistol matches. Pay attention to how shooters adapt their techniques to the specifics of their discipline. For instance, in shotgun sports, see how competitors read the trajectory of clays and adjust their lead to hit moving targets.
- **Positioning and Stance:** Examine how professional shooters position themselves, whether in standing, kneeling, prone, or unconventional positions. Notice how they adjust their stances to maintain stability and accuracy, and how they handle transitions between positions.

2. Strategic and Tactical Insights

- **Competition Strategy:** Professional shooters often develop specific strategies for each competition, including how they plan to approach each stage or series of targets. Observe how they assess the course of fire, plan their movements, and prioritize targets. Analyze their decision-making processes, such as choosing when

to reload, how to approach complex sequences, or how to manage time constraints.
- **Adapting to Conditions:** Watch how professionals adapt to varying conditions such as wind, light changes, or unexpected equipment malfunctions. For instance, observe how a shooter adjusts their hold for wind drift or compensates for glare affecting their sight picture.
- **Handling Pressure:** Study how top shooters manage pressure during critical moments, such as final rounds or tie-breaking scenarios. Pay attention to their body language, breathing techniques, and how they maintain focus despite high stakes.

3. Analyzing Competition Outcomes

- **Success and Areas for Improvement:** Analyze the outcomes of both successful and less successful performances to understand what factors contributed to the results. Break down the elements that led to high scores, such as flawless execution of fundamentals, efficient movement, and optimal equipment choices.
- **Post-Competition Reflections:** Post-competition interviews and debriefs often provide valuable insights into a shooter's mindset and strategy. Pay attention to how professionals reflect on their performance, discuss what worked, and identify what they would change. These reflections can offer additional perspectives on approaches to competition preparation and execution.

REVIEWING YOUR OWN COMPETITIONS: KEY FOCUS AREAS

Reviewing your own performance is essential for identifying strengths, weaknesses, and areas for improvement. Here's an in-depth approach to analyzing your competitive experiences:

1. Technical Execution

- **Shot Accuracy and Consistency:** Evaluate how accurately and consistently you executed your shots throughout the competition. Look for patterns in your performance, such as consistent misses in the same direction or variability in shot placement. Assess whether your fundamentals—such as sight alignment, trigger control, and follow-through—were consistently applied. Identifying specific technical flaws allows for targeted improvement in practice.
- **Positioning:** Analyze your movement between shooting positions and how efficiently you transitioned from one stance to another. Determine if your positioning allowed for stable, accurate shots or if adjustments are needed to improve stability and speed. Efficient movement and positioning are vital for dynamic shooting events where time and accuracy are critical.

2. Tactical Decisions

- **Adherence to Strategy:** Assess how well you followed your pre-competition strategy. Review whether you executed your planned approach to each stage or if deviations occurred. Identify any tactical adjustments you made on the fly and how they affected your overall performance. Understanding the impact of your tactical decisions help refine your strategy for the future competitions.

3. Emotional and Mental Management

- **Composure and Focus:** Reflect on your emotional state throughout the competition. Consider whether you maintained composure and focus or if nerves or frustration impacted your performance. Identifying emotional triggers and stress points allows you to develop mental conditioning techniques to enhance your focus and resilience in future events.
- **Decision-Making Under Pressure:** Analyze your decision-making processes during critical moments. Improving your decision-making skills involves practicing under simulated pressure and learning to make effective choices in real-time.

LEARNING FROM SETBACKS AND ADVERSITY

Setbacks and adversity are part of the journey in shooting sports and provide valuable learning experiences. Here's how to approach and learn from these challenges:

1. Analyzing Setbacks

- **Objective Review:** Review setbacks objectively, focusing on specific aspects of your performance that contributed to the outcome. Avoid blaming external factors and instead focus on what you can control and improve. Objectively analyzing setbacks helps you identify areas for growth and informs your approach to future competitions.

14

THE FUTURE OF SHOOTING SPORTS

SHOOTING SPORTS, WITH A STORIED LEGACY AND A rich tradition, are steadily evolving as they move into the future. From advancements in techniques and training methods to the profound impact of technology and the increasing globalization of the sport, shooting is undergoing significant transformations. This chapter delves into these developments, providing a comprehensive look at how shooting sports are changing and what the future may hold for this dynamic and precise field.

HK Pistol Shoot Naval Base Range

THE PROGRESSION OF SHOOTING TECHNIQUES

- **Contemporary Techniques and Strategies**
  - *Enhancement of Proficiency*
    - *Refinement of Skills*: Shooting techniques have continuously evolved, with modern shooters integrating advanced skills and strategies. Athletes now employ a mix of traditional methods and innovative approaches to elevate their performance. This includes advancements in trigger control, stance optimization, and precision aiming, all of which are refined through meticulous practice and analysis.
    - *Evolving Training Practices*: Training methodologies have also seen considerable advancement, with an increased focus on specific skill development and tactical preparation. Shooters now utilize sophisticated drills and simulation exercises to enhance their accuracy and adaptability in various shooting

1965 European Shooting Championships, Bucharest

scenarios. The integration of these new training methods allow athletes to stay competitive and versatile across different shooting disciplines.

THE ROLE OF TECHNOLOGY IN TRAINING AND PERFORMANCE

- **Technological Innovations**
  - *Advanced Training Tools*
    - *Wearable Technology*: The use of wearable technology, such as smart trackers and biometric sensors, has become commonplace in shooting training. These devices provide crucial data on an athlete's performance, including heart rate, muscle fatigue, and shot timing. This information allows trainers and shooters to make informed decisions about their training regimes, ensuring optimal performance.
    - *Virtual Reality (VR) and Augmented Reality (AR)*: VR and AR technologies are increasingly being utilized to simulate shooting scenarios and enhance training experiences. Shooters can employ VR to practice techniques, visualize complex shooting situations, and improve their reaction times in a controlled environment. AR applications, on the other hand, can provide real-time feedback and augment training sessions with interactive elements that challenge and refine an athlete's skills.
- **Digital Analyze and Simulation**
  - *Enhanced Performance Evaluation*

- *Video Analyze*: Digital video analysis tools allow shooters and coaches to review training sessions and competition footage in detail. This technology enables a comprehensive breakdown of techniques, the identification of strengths and weaknesses, and the development of strategies based on empirical data. Video analysis provides a nuanced understanding of performance, facilitating targeted improvements.

Manu Bhaker with the bronze medal (10m air pistol event, Paris Olympics 2024)

- *Simulation Software*: Simulation software is being used to create virtual shooting scenarios and analyze different shooting styles. This technology helps shooters prepare for various competitions and adapt their strategies accordingly.

THE FUTURE OF SHOOTING SPORTS

LT Amber English wins gold in skeet at 2020 Summer Olympic Games

Simulations offer insights into potential outcomes and allow for precise, targeted preparation.

Most importantly, mastering the basic shooting techniques and combinations is crucial for any aspiring shooter. The stance, grip, sight alignment, trigger control, and follow-through form the core of your shooting skills, while effective combinations enable you to engage targets efficiently and accurately. Through consistent practice and targeted drills, you can enhance your technique, control, and confidence, setting the stage for success in any shooting discipline. As you develop your skills, remember that perfecting these basics is the key to becoming a proficient and formidable shooter in your chosen sport.

15

NURTURING THE NEXT OLYMPIC SHOOTER

AIMING FOR THE OLYMPIC PODIUM

Developing a future Olympic shooter involves unwavering commitment, precision, and comprehensive support. Shooting is a highly technical sport that demands a perfect blend of mental focus, physical control, and the discipline to achieve near-flawless execution under pressure. For young athletes, the road to Olympic-level shooting is long and rigorous yet filled with moments of growth and success. Here's how you can support your aspiring shooter on their journey to becoming a top-tier competitor.

TAKING AIM EARLY: SETTING THE TARGET

Introducing a young athlete to shooting sports early—typically around the age of 8 to 10—helps develop the critical skills of concentration, hand-eye coordination, and steady control. At this stage, focus on creating a safe, fun, and encouraging environment where your child can explore the sport without feeling pressure to compete. Allow them to practice basic shooting techniques with air rifles or air pistols under the guidance of experienced coaches.

Choosing a shooting club or range with certified coaches who understand youth development in the sport is crucial. Look for a facility emphasizing safety, technical skill-building, and fostering a love for shooting over immediate competitive success.

HONING PASSION: KEEPING IT ON TARGET WITHOUT OVERLOADING THE SIGHTS

While investing time in shooting is essential, allow your young athlete to explore other activities. Cross-training with sports such as archery or athletics can enhance their overall athletic ability and mental focus and help avoid burnout. Shooting is a sport that requires immense patience and precision, so keeping their experience varied and exciting is crucial in developing a well-rounded competitor.

Celebrate incremental improvements, whether mastering the fundamentals of trigger control or achieving a consistent grouping on the target. Focusing on personal milestones over competition outcomes will instill resilience and help them maintain a positive connection with the sport.

SHARPSHOOTING TRAINING: FINDING THE RIGHT SCOPE

As your child progresses, their training regimen must become more structured and intense. Early competitors (ages 10-12) may start training once or twice a week, increasing to multiple sessions as they advance. By their teenage years, aspiring Olympians might spend up to 30 hours a week perfecting their aim, form, and focus. Ensuring a balance in their training program will prevent overuse injuries and mental fatigue.

Expert coaching is vital at this stage. Seek out instructors with a deep understanding of the nuances of competitive shooting. They should be capable of guiding the athlete through advanced technical skills, mental training for precision under pressure, and strategies to remain calm and composed in high-stakes situations.

FUELLING THE SHOT: NUTRITION AND RECOVERY FOR SHOOTERS

Supporting high-level shooting requires optimal nutrition. Shooters must maintain sharp focus for extended periods, so a balanced diet of lean proteins, complex carbohydrates, healthy fats, and nutrient-rich vegetables is essential. Adequate hydration, especially during long training sessions or competitions, is equally important for maintaining focus and reaction time.

Recovery is crucial for any athlete, and shooters are no exception. Ensure your child gets sufficient sleep and takes rest days to allow for mental rejuvenation. In a sport requiring precise control, recovery from physical and mental fatigue is essential to maintain peak performance. Incorporate relaxation techniques or light physical conditioning to manage tension and sustain agility.

TRIGGERING SUCCESS: INJURY PREVENTION AND PROPER SHOOTING TECHNIQUE

Injury prevention in shooting often centers around proper technique and form. Coaches should maintain correct posture, grip, and breathing techniques to avoid strain or injury, particularly in the shoulders, back, and neck. Overtraining can lead to fatigue, affecting accuracy and performance, so a well-rounded training plan is critical.

If any physical discomfort or injury arises, address it immediately. Continuing to train with poor form or through pain can lead to long-term issues. Consult a sports medicine specialist familiar with the demands of shooting to create a recovery plan, and only return to full training when fully healed.

ON-TARGET AND OFF-BALANCING SHOOTING WITH LIFE

Balancing training with academics and social activities becomes crucial as your child progresses in competitive shooting. Effective time management will ensure they don't become overwhelmed by the demands of high-level competition. Encourage hobbies and friendships outside the sport to create a well-rounded, happy individual.

The path to Olympic success in shooting is a marathon, requiring patience and perseverance. Celebrate your child's sports growth, whether mastering a new skill or hitting a personal best score. Fostering a positive and supportive environment at home will ensure that they stay motivated and enthusiastic throughout their journey.

16

FILIPINO OLYMPIANS IN SHOOTING SPORTS

FILIPINO SHOOTERS HAVE SHOWCASED THEIR dedication, skill, and precision. The governing body responsible for developing and promoting shooting sports in the Philippines is the Philippine National Shooting Association (PNSA), which plays a pivotal role in nurturing athletes and preparing them for both Olympic and non-Olympic competitions.

The Philippine National Shooting Association (PNSA), headquartered in Pasig, Metro Manila, is the National Sports Association (NSA) for shooting sports in the country. It oversees a wide array of shooting disciplines, including Olympic shooting events like pistol, rifle, and shotgun, as well as non-Olympic events such as practical pistol and bench rest shooting. The PNSA is recognized by the Philippine Olympic Committee (POC) and is funded by the Philippine Sports Commission (PSC), allowing it to support the development of elite athletes and facilities across the nation.

As a member of the International Shooting Sport

Federation (ISSF), the global governing body for shooting sports, the PNSA aligns itself with international standards, ensuring that Filipino athletes are competitive on the world stage. It is also an accredited member of the Asian Shooting Confederation (ASC) and the Asian Clay Shooting Federation, further embedding itself in the international shooting community.

In the pursuit of excellence, the PNSA has developed world-class training facilities, most notably the PNSA-PSC Shooting Ranges in Fort Bonifacio, Taguig City. These ranges cater to events across 10m, 25m, and 50m distances, and are used by both professional and youth shooters. For Trap and Skeet events, Filipino shooters train at the PNSA Clay Target Range in Muntinlupa, which has hosted international competitions, including the 2005 Southeast Asian Games.

Shooter Jayson Valdez

A significant milestone in Filipino shooting sports came in 2012, when the 10m Air Shooting Range in Fort Bonifacio was equipped with an electronic target system. The ISSF Rule Changes for 2013-2016 introduced decimal scoring.

One of the key components of the PNSA's athlete development program is the National Open, an annual series of shooting events that attract top Filipino talent. Both youth and adult shooters compete in this prestigious event, with the best performers earning spots in the National Training Pool. These athletes receive critical support, including ammunition, allowances, and access to advanced training facilities, preparing them for the rigors of international competition.

To qualify for international events, Filipino shooters must meet their discipline's Minimum Qualification Scores (MQS), which are benchmarked against the bronze medal score from the last Asian Games. Those who meet the MQS are selected to compete in a range of events, from regional competitions like the Southeast Asian Games (SEA Games) and Asian Games to world-level tournaments such as the ISSF World Cups and World Championships.

Notable Filipino shooters like Martin Gison, who competed in the 1972 Munich Olympics, have paved the way for the country's current crop of elite marksmen.

Today, athletes like Franchette Quiroz and Amparo Acuna are leading the charge for the Philippines in the race for Olympic qualification. Quiroz, in particular, has made waves in the international shooting community with her performances in the 25m air pistol event. Training under Qatari coach Murad Hanov, Quiroz has set new national records and steadily climbed the world rankings, positioning herself as a strong contender for a place in the 2024 Paris Olympics.

Shooter Martin Mauricio Gison

Acuna, meanwhile, has shown similar promise, making it to the finals of the 25m action event in the Jakarta Olympic qualifier.

The PNSA has also demonstrated its commitment to inclusivity through its partnership with PhilSPADA, the Philippine Sports Association for Differently Abled Athletes. This collaboration allows athletes with disabilities to participate in Paralympic shooting events, using the same equipment as their able-bodied counterparts, with minor modifications such as shooting tables and chairs. Filipino Paralympic shooters are now competing on the world stage, using the same classification system as the International Paralympic Committee Shooting (IPC Shooting).

LIST OF OLYMPIC MEDALISTS IN SHOOTING (2008–2024)

Men Air pistol

Games	Gold	Silver	Bronze
2016 Rio de Janeiro	Hoàng Xuân Vinh Vietnam	Felipe Wu Brazil	Pang Wei China
2020 Tokyo	Javad Foroughi Iran	Damir Mikec Serbia	Pang Wei China
2024 Paris	Xie Yu China	Federico Nilo Maldini Italy	Paolo Monna Italy

Men Air rifle

Games	Gold	Silver	Bronze
2008 Beijing	Abhinav Bindra India	Zhu Qinan China	Henri Häkkinen Finland
2012 London	Alin Moldoveanu Romania	Niccolò Campriani Italy	Gagan Narang India
2016 Rio de Janeiro	Niccolò Campriani Italy	Serhiy Kulish Ukraine	Vladimir Maslennikov Russia

LIST OF OLYMPIC MEDALISTS (2008-2024)

Games	Gold	Silver	Bronze
2020 Tokyo	Will Shaner 🇺🇸 United States	Sheng Lihao 🇨🇳 China	Yang Haoran 🇨🇳 China
2024 Paris	Sheng Lihao 🇨🇳 China	Victor Lindgren 🇸🇪 Sweden	Miran Maričić 🇭🇷 Croatia

Men Rapid fire pistol

Games	Gold	Silver	Bronze
2012 London	Leuris Pupo 🇨🇺 Cuba	Vijay Kumar 🇮🇳 India	Ding Feng 🇨🇳 China
2016 Rio de Janeiro	Christian Reitz 🇩🇪 Germany	Jean Quiquampoix 🇫🇷 France	Li Yuehong 🇨🇳 China
2020 Tokyo	Jean Quiquampoix 🇫🇷 France	Leuris Pupo 🇨🇺 Cuba	Li Yuehong 🇨🇳 China
2024 Paris	Li Yuehong 🇨🇳 China	Cho Yeong-jae 🇰🇷 South Korea	Wang Xinjie 🇨🇳 China

Men Rifle three positions

Games	Gold	Silver	Bronze
2012 London	Niccolò Campriani 🇮🇹 Italy	Kim Jong-hyun 🇰🇷 South Korea	Matthew Emmons 🇺🇸 United States
2016 Rio de Janeiro	Niccolò Campriani 🇮🇹 Italy	Sergey Kamenskiy 🇷🇺 Russia	Alexis Raynaud 🇫🇷 France
2020 Tokyo	Zhang Changhong 🇨🇳 China	Sergey Kamenskiy ROC	Milenko Sebić 🇷🇸 Serbia
2024 Paris	Liu Yukun 🇨🇳 China	Serhiy Kulish 🇺🇦 Ukraine	Swapnil Kusale 🇮🇳 India

Skeet

Games	Gold	Silver	Bronze
2012 London	Vincent Hancock — United States	Anders Golding — Denmark	Nasser Al-Attiyah — Qatar
2016 Rio de Janeiro	Gabriele Rossetti — Italy	Marcus Svensson — Sweden	Abdullah Al-Rashidi — Independent Olympic Athletes
2020 Tokyo	Vincent Hancock — United States	Jesper Hansen — Denmark	Abdullah Al-Rashidi — Kuwait
2024 Paris	Vincent Hancock — United States	Conner Prince — United States	Lee Meng-yuan — Chinese Taipei

Trap

Games	Gold	Silver	Bronze
2012 London	Giovanni Cernogoraz — Croatia	Massimo Fabbrizi — Italy	Fehaid Al-Deehani — Kuwait
2016 Rio de Janeiro	Josip Glasnović — Croatia	Giovanni Pellielo — Italy	Edward Ling — Great Britain
2020 Tokyo	Jiří Lipták — Czech Republic	David Kostelecký — Czech Republic	Matthew Coward-Holley — Great Britain
2024 Paris	Nathan Hales — Great Britain	Qi Ying — China	Jean Pierre Brol — Guatemala

Women Air Pistol

Games	Gold	Silver	Bronze
2012 London	Guo Wenjun, China	Céline Goberville, France	Olena Kostevych, Ukraine
2016 Rio de Janeiro	Zhang Mengxue, China	Vitalina Batsarashkina, Russia	Anna Korakaki, Greece
2020 Tokyo	Vitalina Batsarashkina, ROC	Antoaenta Kostadinova, Bulgaria	Jiang Ranxin, China
2024 Paris	Oh Ye-jin, South Korea	Kim Ye-ji, South Korea	Manu Bhaker, India

Women Air rifle

Games	Gold	Silver	Bronze
2012 London	Yi Siling, China	Sylwia Bogacka, Poland	Yu Dan, China
2016 Rio de Janeiro	Virginia Thrasher, United States	Du Li, China	Yi Siling, China
2020 Tokyo	Yang Qian, China	Anastasiia Galashina, ROC	Nina Christen, Switzerland
2024 Paris	Ban Hyo-jin, South Korea	Huang Yuting, China	Audrey Gogniat, Switzerland

Women (Sport) Pistol

Games	Gold	Silver	Bronze
2012 London	Kim Jang-mi South Korea	Chen Ying China	Olena Kostevych Ukraine
2016 Rio de Janeiro	Anna Korakaki Greece	Monika Karsch Germany	Heidi Diethelm Gerber Switzerland
2020 Tokyo	Vitalina Batsarashkina ROC	Kim Min-jung South Korea	Xiao Jiaruixuan China
2024 Paris	Yang Ji-in South Korea	Camille Jedrzejewski France	Veronika Major Hungary

Women Rifle three positions (standard rifle and sport rifle)

Games	Gold	Silver	Bronze
2012 London	Jamie Lynn Gray United States	Ivana Maksimović Serbia	Adéla Sýkorová Czech Republic
2016 Rio de Janeiro	Barbara Engleder Germany	Zhang Binbin China	Du Li China
2020 Tokyo	Nina Christen Switzerland	Yulia Zykova ROC	Yulia Karimova ROC
2024 Paris	Chiara Leone Switzerland	Sagen Maddalena United States	Zhang Qiongyue China

Women Skeet

Games	Gold	Silver	Bronze
2016 Rio de Janeiro	Diana Bacosi Italy	Chiara Cainero Italy	Kim Rhode United States
2020 Tokyo	Amber English United States	Diana Bacosi Italy	Wei Meng China
2024 Paris	Francisca Crovetto Chile	Amber Rutter Great Britain	Austen Smith United States

Women Trap

Games	Gold	Silver	Bronze
2016 Rio de Janeiro	Catherine Skinner Australia	Natalie Rooney New Zealand	Corey Cogdell United States
2020 Tokyo	Zuzana Rehák-Štefečeková Slovakia	Kayle Browning United States	Alessandra Perilli San Marino
2024 Paris	Adriana Ruano Guatemala	Silvana Stanco Italy	Penny Smith Australia

Mixed Air pistol, team

Games	Gold	Silver	Bronze
2020 Tokyo	China (CHN) Jiang Ranxin Pang Wei	ROC (ROC) Vitalina Batsarashkina Artem Chernousov	Ukraine (UKR) Olena Kostevych Oleh Omelchuk

Games	Gold	Silver	Bronze
2024 Paris	Serbia (SRB) Zorana Arunović Damir Mikec	Turkey (TUR) Şevval İlayda Tarhan Yusuf Dikeç	India (IND) Manu Bhaker Sarabjot Singh

Air rifle, team

Games	Gold	Silver	Bronze
2020 Tokyo	China (CHN) Yang Qian Yang Haoran	United States (USA) Mary Tucker Lucas Kozeniesky	ROC (ROC) Yulia Karimova Sergey Kamenskiy
2024 Paris	China (CHN) Huang Yuting Sheng Lihao	South Korea (KOR) Keum Ji-hyeon Park Ha-jun	Kazakhstan (KAZ) Alexandra Le Islam Satpayev

Skeet, team

Games	Gold	Silver	Bronze
2024 Paris	Italy (ITA) Diana Bacosi Gabriele Rossetti	United States (USA) Austen Smith Vincent Hancock	China (CHN) Jiang Yiting Lyu Jianlin